JOSSEY-BASS TEACHER

Jossey-Bass Teacher provides educators with practical knowledge and tools to create a positive and lifelong impact on student learning. We offer classroom-tested and research-based teaching resources for a variety of grade levels and subject areas. Whether you are an aspiring, new, or veteran teacher, we want to help you make every teaching day your best.

From ready-to-use classroom activities to the latest teaching framework, our value-packed books provide insightful, practical, and comprehensive materials on the topics that matter most to K–12 teachers. We hope to become your trusted source for the best ideas from the most experienced and respected experts in the field.

The **READING** Teacher's WORD-A-DAY

180 Ready-to-Use Lessons to Expand Vocabulary, Teach Roots, and Prepare for Standardized Tests

Edward B. Fry, Ph.D.

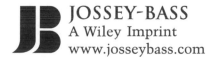

JOSSEY-BASS
A Wiley Imprint
www.josseybass.com

THE AUTHOR

Edward B. Fry, Ph.D., is Professor Emeritus of Education at Rutgers University (New Brunswick, NJ) where for twenty-four years he was director of the Reading Center. At Rutgers, Dr. Fry taught graduate and undergraduate courses in reading, curriculum, and other educational subjects, and served as chairman and dissertation committee member for doctoral candidates in reading and educational psychology. As the Reading Center's director, he provided instruction for children with reading problems, trained teacher candidates, and conducted statewide reading conferences. Author of the best-selling book, *The Reading Teacher's Book of Lists,* Dr. Fry is known internationally for his Readability Graph, which is used by teachers, publishers, and others to judge the reading difficulty of books and other materials. He is also well known for his Instant Words, high-frequency word list; and for reading, spelling, and secondary curriculum materials. He works as a curriculum author and skis and swims whenever possible.

ACKNOWLEDGMENTS

I would like to thank William Nagy of Seattle Pacific University for getting me a copy of and suggesting that I read the now-out-of-print technical report of the University of Oregon's morphograph study (see Appendix B and the References). I would also like to acknowledge the valuable help of my editorial assistant, Julie Josephson, who worked on the manuscript in many ways, and the writing help of my granddaughter Brandie Schafer, a star secondary language arts teacher, who wrote a few of the lessons.

E. F.

CONTENTS

How to Use This Book   xv
Lessons

_____

Contents

HOW TO USE THIS BOOK

The title of this book gives you the basic idea of its purpose: *learn one word a day*.

Ah, but what does it mean to *learn* a word?

Does it mean to be able to *read* it aloud (pronounce it)?

Does it mean to know one or two short *definitions*?

Does it mean to be able to *use it* in a sentence?

Does it mean to know some *related words* (similar roots)?

Does it mean to be able to write (*spell*) the word?

You decide. This book will help you in any or all of these areas.

There are 180 lessons in this book, and it just so happens that there are about 180 days in the school year.

This book can be used in school or out of school for self-study, tutoring, or home schooling.

Some students will use this book to prepare for an upcoming examination. Most tests—from the state tests in middle school to the Scholastic Achievement Test to the Graduate Record Exam and many others—include vocabulary.

But more important than test scores is becoming an educated person, and a good vocabulary is certainly a hallmark of an educated person. It shows up in speaking, in writing, and in reading and listening comprehension.

Some Ideas for the Teacher

The teacher can use this book a little or a lot. You can use the words in this book for some incidental teaching about vocabulary or you can incorporate a serious vocabulary strand in your curriculum for the year.

Select one or more of the following levels or vary the level according to your interest in the word or the time available.

The lessons may be done in any order. You can start with lesson 1 or with a lesson in the middle; you can skip around randomly or pick lessons related to the other topics in your curriculum.

Here is just one way to use this book:

Level 1: Light Touch—Three Minutes a Day

The students walk into class and instead of just chatting, they look at a corner section of the board to see the Word of the Day and then write it down in their notebooks. The teacher then calls attention to the word, pronounces it correctly and syllable by syllable, tells the students the meaning, and maybe directs a small amount of discussion about it. The word remains on the board all day.

Level 2: Roots

Extending the discussion five minutes longer includes pointing out the word's root and how the same root is used in related words. Frequently the prefix or suffix is given for the main word and for the related words. The related words are often more common words, but the student might not be aware that they have the same root.

Level 3: Activities

Add three to five minutes to the discussion to use the activities mentioned on each lesson page. The activities are designed to engender thinking about the word and may be used for student discussion or occasionally for a written assignment.

Level 4: Spelling

Spelling is optional and incorporating it into the lesson adds a bit more time, but if you expect the students to use the vocabulary word of the day in writing, it is essential to know how to spell it. Writing the word in a spelling lesson also helps to ensure that the word is learned. Spelling lessons are not often taught systematically in the upper grades, but the words offered here may be the basis of an advanced spelling curriculum.

Ask the students to study the word of the day. Be sure they know how each syllable is pronounced and spelled (the phonetic spelling is given at the top of the page, the correct spelling of the syllables is given at the bottom; *urge the students to pay attention to each syllable* when studying the word for correct spelling). They should then try to write the word without copying (without looking at the written word). If they make mistakes, study the mistakes.

Review

Review helps all learning. On Friday, review the week's words using Level 1, 2, 3, or 4. This could be a self-corrected spelling test. Reviewing the words again after a longer period, such as a month or a semester, is also good.

Learning

How students learn anything is interesting and elusive but here are some suggestions that can be found in many educational psychology books.

Attention is basic. One of the first steps in any learning effort is simply to pay attention to what should be learned. The discussion and activities help the students to focus their attention on the word.

Level 1 takes advantage of different forms of sensory input. The students *see* the word, they *hear* it pronounced, and they *write* it.

The first three levels together then pile on *meaning* and offer *association* hooks. This often amounts to the expansion of previous partial knowledge of meaning into a more mature knowledge of the word. Note the earlier review paragraph, which suggests that learning can be aided by reviewing previous lessons.

Goals

Many of the words presented here will be new to the students (and occasionally to the teacher), yet only part of the purpose of teaching them is to introduce them to the students. Even more important is to develop the students' interest in words, in their meaning, derivation, and relatives.

By learning many word roots, the student will see that knowing and looking for roots aids the lifelong interesting task of learning new words.

Knowing the meaning of words (vocabulary) is basic to reading comprehension, so another major goal is to improve reading comprehension.

An additional goal is to improve writing skills. Good, interesting writers have an extensive vocabulary.

Finally, having strong vocabulary skills will help students improve their scores on standardized tests.

Pedagogy

This is an old-fashioned book; it needs a teacher. It does not include a workbook or duplicatable worksheets (although you can duplicate any page for students in your class). You do not need a computer or audiovisual equipment. However, a chalkboard and student notebooks would be helpful.

Some self-motivated students will want to improve their vocabulary; you can just hand these students the book.

Be Creative

These teaching suggestions are just that: suggestions.

Use this book in any way you want. Some teachers will start with the first lesson and do them all in order; others will skip a lesson and jump to one more interesting or appropriate. Some teachers will do just Level 1, introducing the basic word for the day, and some will do all four levels, right up through spelling.

This book contains a whole bucket of tools for teaching vocabulary. Use all or some of these tools, but whatever you do, teach vocabulary. It is one of the most important things you can do.

—Edward Fry

P.S. Don't forget to look at the Appendixes;
there are some interesting things there.
See especially the comments on page 181.

The READING Teacher's WORD-A-DAY

1 vocation /vo kay shun /vō kā' shən

A *vocation* is a person's main occupation, job, or employment.
It is often used in a religious sense to indicate a *calling* (inclination) to the ministry or priesthood. But it is also used to describe any occupation that requires dedication, such as nursing or teaching. It is not wrong to say that a plumber has a *vocation*, but plumbing is more often called a job, a trade, or a craft.

Root
voc means "call."

A *vocation* is usually a paid full-time occupation. In contrast, an *avocation* is usually a nonpaid, often part-time occupation or hobby. For example, watching birds and knowing about birds is an *avocation* for most people, but for an ornithologist (a scientist who studies birds) it is a *vocation*. The prefix *a-* in this case means "not."

vocabulary – a collection of words, the number of words known by an individual, or words used in a particular subject area: "Music has its own *vocabulary*."

vocal cords – the part of the throat that makes sounds, a membrane that vibrates with the passage of air.

vocalist – a person who sings: "The band members who sing are its *vocalists*."

vocalize – to put into words or to speak: "She couldn't *vocalize* her real feelings."

vociferous – loud or insistent speech: "Blue Jays have a *vociferous* call."

equivocate – to speak on both sides of an issue, to avoid making a definite decision, not to make up one's mind. (*equi-* = equal)

Activities

A girl who sings with a band
is a _____.

Someone who talks all the time and won't shut
up is _____.

Name some actions that are *irrevocable* (that
can't be undone).

If you don't get paid for doing it, it might be
an _____.

Syllabification for correct spelling

_____
vo-ca-tion

2 worst /werst /wûrst

The common meaning of *worst* is "very bad"—in fact, as bad as bad can get.

The adjective *bad* has three degrees. The first degree, *bad,* is known as the *positive* degree and is the simple and most commonly used form of the word. The next degree, *worse,* is known as the comparative degree. And finally, *worst* is known as the superlative degree. For example, "The storm was already bad, it got worse an hour later, but the next day it was the *worst* I have ever seen."

Most adjectives are regular and are changed simply by adding a suffix, as in *big, bigger, biggest.* Only a few adjectives, such as *bad, worse,* and *worst,* are *irregular.* Other examples include:

| good | better | best |
| many | more | most |

Some tricky tests, such as the SAT, may use an obscure meaning for a common word. *Worst,* for example, may be used as a verb meaning "to defeat," "to outdo," or "to best in a debate or conflict": "My attorney tried to *worst* the prosecution attorney" or "Our army was *worsted* (defeated) in the battle."

Activities

Here are some adjectives in the positive degree. Put them in the comparative and superlative degrees:

small _____

_____

dirty _____

_____

worried* _____

_____

many _____

_____

*requires *more* or *most*

> **Syllabification for correct spelling**
>
> _____
>
> **worst**

3 catalyst /cat a list /kat' l ist

A *catalyst* is a substance that can cause a reaction. For example, some modern cars have a *catalyst* in the car engine exhaust muffler that causes some of the gas emitted from the engine's exhaust to be less toxic (harmful).

A *catalyst* can also be something that causes other kinds of change. For example, Congress could pass a bill (law) that would make it easier for people to have solar energy for their houses. Such a bill would be a *catalyst* for change from using power made by oil-fired electricity-generating plants to using free solar energy (sunshine) to make electricity. The solar generator uses silicon cells as *catalysts* for changing solar radiation into electricity. (-*lyst* = breakdown)

Root
cata **means "with."**

catastrophe – a tragedy, disaster, or utter failure: "A hurricane is a *catastrophe*." (*trophe-* = turn) *Catastrophe* is an ancient Greek term meaning "The gods have turned against us."

catalog – a list or book of various items, such as a college *catalog* of courses or a store *catalog* of items for sale. (-*log* = word)

catapult – an ancient war machine for hurling stones. (*pult-* = hurl)

Activities

Does *catalyst* have anything to do with cats?

Does *catalyst* have anything to do with hurricanes?

Does *catalyst* have anything to do with chemistry?

Does *catalyst* have anything to do with modern society?

Syllabification for correct spelling

_____

cat-a-lyst

4 countervail /cown ter vail /koun' tər vāl'

The word *countervail* means "to oppose or exert a force against" something: "The enemy had a *countervailing* force protecting the river." "*Countervailing* his tendency to love was his tendency to hate."

Countervail also has another meaning: *to compensate* or *to make up for*. For example, "She *countervailed* for the tree damage by planting a new tree."

counterweight – a weight equal or opposing: "An old scale had a *counterweight* and some elevators and windows had *counterweights*." "The courts acted as a *counterweight* to the legislature."

counterthrust – an opposing force: "Rockets and springs can exert a *counterthrust*."

counterview – a view or argument from the opposite side.

countermand – to recall or cancel an order.

encounter – to meet face-to-face, to meet the enemy, to come upon accidentally.

counterclockwise – movement from the top of a circle to the left, turning the opposite way a clock dial runs.

Activities

In what other situations might you use *countervail*?

Draw a picture of the use of a *counterweight*.

Review: What does *counter-* mean?

If you *countermand* an order, what does that mean?

Syllabification for correct spelling

_____

coun-ter-vail

5 fluid /floo id /flōo' id

Fluid is a common word with several meanings:

1. a liquid substance (noun): "My car needed both *brake fluid* and *radiator fluid*."

2. not fixed, changing (adj.): "The battle lines were so *fluid* that they changed from day to day." "His opinion of the president was *fluid* and changed with every newspaper article."

3. a smooth or easy style (adj.): "The best dancers have very *fluid* movements."

4. easily converted to cash (adj.): "Government bonds are *fluid* and can be sold for cash any time you wish. They have *fluidity*."

Root
flu comes from Latin and means "flow" or "blow."

All sorts of things are *fluid* and *flow;* besides water, gas *flows* through pipes to our stoves, electricity *flows* through copper wire to our lightbulbs, mud *flows* down wet mountain sides, and even ice *flows* down glaciers.

flue – a pipe for venting gases, as in a chimney; historically a *flue* was an open wooden or stone trough for carrying water.

fluff – a lightweight substance with air between the particles; you can *fluff* a food, such as whipped cream, or *fluff* up a pillow.

flow – current or movement of a liquid or gas: "Which way does the river *flow*?"

affluent – wealthy, rich, flowing in abundance.

Activities

Name ten kinds of *fluid*.

What does *fluidity* mean?

Use *fluff* in several ways.

What else *flows* in addition to liquid?

Syllabification for correct spelling

---

flu-id

6 triad /try add /trī' ad

A *triad* is any group of three closely related things or people: "Those three political leaders are a *triad*; they all vote the same way." "A *triad* is a musical chord consisting of three tones."

triangle – a plane geometric figure with three angles and three sides.

> **right triangle** – a triangle with one angle at 90 degrees.

> **isosceles triangle** – a triangle with two sides of equal length. (*iso-* = equal)

> **equilateral triangle** – a triangle with all sides of equal length.

> [In some words, *-lateral* means "side." A *lateral pass* in football is a pass sideways rather than forward. A *lateral branch* is one that grows from the side of a main branch. Pipelines and electrical lines have *laterals* (lateral branches) coming off the main lines.]

trident – a three-tooth spear; a symbol of the sea god Neptune.

tribe – a large family or clan; related families; a group united under one chief; a group of animals. Historically, a *tribe* was a division of one third of the Roman people.

Root
tri means "three."

Activities

Draw some differently shaped *right triangles*.

Draw some differently shaped *isosceles triangles*.

How many *laterals* does a *triangle* have?

What is the symbol for Neptune, the sea god?

Syllabification for correct spelling

————————

tri-ad

Do *unemphatic* and *unequivocal* /un ee kwiv ik ull/ mean the same thing? Heavens, no. To *equivocate* means to avoid making a decision or to speak on both sides of an issue, so *unequivocal* means your mind is made up—no more questioning or hesitation. *Unemphatic* means "without emphasis or strong meaning." When you *emphasize* something, you call attention to it or put it in a position of importance; put *un-* in front of *emphatic* and it means *not emphatic*, or not important. "She spoke *unemphatically* when denying that she would run for office" (meaning she won't run).

It means "not" or "opposite." We see it in hundreds of words in the dictionary, such as:

Prefix

un is the most common prefix in the English language.

unrest	unconstitutional	ungraceful
unwarlike	unchosen	undressed

And it can *unofficially* be applied to many slang words:

uncool   unhip   unmacho

The prefix *in-* may also mean "not," as in:

inattention   inaccurate   indirect

Also the prefix *im-* means "not," as in:

impossible   impolite   improbable

And the prefix *ir-* means "not," as in:

irregular   irresistible   irrelevant

Activities

Is a person who cannot make up his or her mind *equivocal* or *unequivocal*?

List four prefixes that mean "not."

When you don't want to emphasize something, do you say it *emphatically* or *unemphatically*?

Try applying *un-* to a variety of words.

Syllabification for correct spelling

─────────────

un-em-phat-ic

Papyrus is the name of a plant famous for growing along the banks of the Nile River in Egypt but that can also be found in many gardens in the United States, particularly those near or with a pond. *Papyrus* is a member of the sedge family, which is noted for having long stocks that are somewhat triangular (three-sided) rather than round.

Historically, *papyrus* was very important because two thousand years ago it was used to make writing paper. In fact, the word *paper* comes from *papyrus*. The ancient Egyptians cut the *papyrus* stalks into long strips and pressed them together to form the paper, which was sometimes made into a long strip and rolled up into a *scroll*. Later it was cut into pages and bound into book form, or *codex*. The codex was a great invention because it made it possible to write on both sides of the *papyrus* paper, and it was easier to use than a scroll.

The term *papyrus* also refers to specific books or manuscripts. For example, the Turin Papyrus of Kings, now housed in the Egyptian Museum in Turin, Italy, lists ancient Egyptian kings. Most of the books of the Bible were originally written on *papyrus*. The older, Jewish books (the Old Testament) were written on scrolls and the newer, Christian books (the New Testament) were usually written in a codex.

Papyrus was used as writing paper not only by the ancient Egyptians but also by the ancient Greeks and Romans (ancient Italians). People who study *papyrus* books are called *papyrologists*.

Activities

Why did the ancient Egyptians write on *papyrus* instead of on paper?

Try writing your next story on a scroll.

Draw a picture of a *papyrus* plant.

What nationality are the ancient Romans called today?

Syllabification for correct spelling
pa-py-rus

9 crude /krewd /kro͞od

Does *crude* sound like *rude*?

Is there any relationship in meaning between the two words?

Yes, there certainly is. A person who is *rude* can also be called *crude*. A rude person is unpolished, impolite, not finished, such as somebody who cuts in front of you when you are in line, or somebody who interrupts your talking by speaking before you have finished. "It's both *rude* and *crude* to make insulting remarks about somebody's handicap."

But *crude* is not always an impolite word. Here are some other meanings:

Root
crudus comes from Latin and means "raw" or "rough."

1. natural, raw, not refined: "*Crude* oil must be sent to a refinery."

2. made quickly or poorly, temporarily, hastily: "He lived in a *crude* cabin in the woods."

3. language or actions that are impolite, insulting, offensive: "He made *crude* jokes about minorities."

4. incomplete or not well thought out: "He had only a *crude* sketch for the building plan."

recrudescent – becoming raw again: "The sore on her foot was *recrudescent*." "There was *recrudescent* discontent among the workers before the strike."

Activities

List five types of *crude* materials.

List five types of *rude* behavior.

Make a *crude* drawing of the floor plan of your bedroom.

What are some words that mean the opposite of *crude*?

Syllabification for correct spelling

_____

crude

10 bedraggle /be drag gull /bi drag' əl

You should always look for the little word or root in long or unfamiliar words. In *bedraggle* we clearly see the word *drag,* and sure enough, that is part of the definition. If someone shows up at your door looking *bedraggled,* he looks as if he has been *dragged.* But he would also be *wet.* So if you say that after a rainstorm your dog looks "wet and *bedraggled,*" you are really repeating yourself.

Bedraggle also has another meaning and that is "to move slowly or perhaps even slovenly." If your teacher takes you to the museum and tries to keep the group together, she might get a little annoyed if a few students *bedraggle,* that is, move to the rear and act as a *drag* for the whole group.

The prefix *be-* is a well-used Old English prefix that is attached to a lot of words. Shakespeare used it all the time and it is still in dozens of modern words.

Be- might be related to position, meaning "on" or "around," as in *beside, behind, below,* and *beyond.*

Be- might help to change a noun into a verb, as in *befriend, behead, bedevil,* and *bewitch.*

Be- might also intensify or make a word stronger, as in *befuddle, berate,* and *beware.*

Here is a simple test to find out whether or not a word is a noun. If you can put "the" in front of the word, it is a noun. For example, you can't say "the befriend," but you can say, "The soldier befriended the young boy." So the prefix *be-* does have a grammar use.

Activities

Describe someone who looks *bedraggled.*

Have you ever seen someone *bedraggle* in a group?

Can you think of another word that uses the prefix *be-?*

> **Syllabification for correct spelling**
> _____
> **be-drag-gle**

11 dictatorial /dik tuh tor ee ul /dik' tə tôr' ē əl

Dictatorial means acting like a dictator, who puts you in prison if you don't agree with him, or like a bad boss whose attitude is "my way or the highway."

There are a number of synonyms for this unflattering word:

domineering	oppressive	overbearing
despotic	tyrannical	autocratic
commanding	absolute	totalitarian

Root
dict comes from Latin and means "to speak."

Use these synonyms often when writing about a person and you mean that person is *dictatorial*.

dictate – to speak as another person writes down what is said; to give orders: "She is always trying to *dictate* to me."

dictionary – a reference book containing a list of words and their meanings.

diction – correctness in choice of words and pronunciation or enunciation: "Actors tend to have good *diction*; people who mumble their spoken words have bad *diction*." "All students should strive to have good *diction*, because it helps the listener at the other end of the cell phone connection."

contradict – to speak against an idea or concept; to take an opposing view. (*contra-* = against)

benediction – to speak well of something or somebody; to give a blessing. (*bene-* = well)

Activities

Use the word *dictatorial* in a sentence, then try using several synonyms in its place.

Say this sentence with good *diction* and with bad *diction*.

Does a *dictator dictate*?

Is a commander always bad?

Syllabification for correct spelling

---

dic-ta-to-ri-al

Exotic has two rather different meanings:

1. foreign or not native. For example, Chinese food is *exotic* in America and hamburgers are *exotic* in China. *Exotic* plants are not native or natural to an area; they originally came from a different place.

2. something quite unusual or different in appearance. For example, dying your hair purple is definitely *exotic*. Wearing a bikini to a dinner party is far-out *exotic,* and bad manners too, but wearing a sari (Indian woman's dress) is *exotic* and can be quite pleasing.

Prefix
ex- is used in many words.

Ex- has several related meanings:

1. *ex-* can mean "out of" or "outside": "The *exterior* of your house is the outside." "An *exit* sign shows you the way out."

2. *ex-* can mean "former," especially with a hyphen, as in *ex-president* and *ex-husband.*

3. *ex-* can mean "beyond." For example, *exceed* means to go beyond the usual limits: "Don't *exceed* the speed limit or you will get a ticket." *Explore* means to move into new territory, new thinking, or new actions: "You can *explore* African jungles or a new house."

Activities

Mention something *exotic* that you have seen recently.

Name an *ex-president* of the United States.

Which meaning—1, 2, or 3—is the meaning of the *ex-* in *explain*?

Which meaning—1, 2, or 3—is the meaning of the *ex-* in *export*?

Syllabification for correct spelling

---

ex-ot-ic

13 imperturbable /im per turb uh bull   /im' pər tûr'bə bəl

Imperturbable means staying calm and steady, not likely to get excited, or as some might express it, "cool." So, if the captain of a sinking ship is still giving calm, rational orders to abandon ship, he is *imperturbable*. (*im-* = not)

perturb – cause to be upset, worried, or alarmed: "When I lose my keys, I'm *perturbed*." (The prefix *per-* is a general intensifier and means something like "thoroughly.")

Root
turb means "to throw into disorder."

disturb – interfere with normal functioning: "The noise *disturbed* my sleep."

undisturbed – left as you found it, unchanged. (*un-* = not)

turbulent – wildly unruly, disorderly, stormy. The weather can be *turbulent* or the political situation can be *turbulent*.

turbine – a rotary engine that is activated by water, gas, steam, or another fluid. Modern large airplanes have *turbine* engines. At dams, electricity is generated by a stream of water falling past a *turbine*.

turbid – cloudy or opaque due to sediment or other particles being stirred up, as in water or air containing fine particles that make it unclear: "He couldn't see the bottom of the stream because the water was so *turbid*."

Activities

What are some situations that *perturb* you?

Describe a situation in which you could have been *perturbed* but were *imperturbable*.

Try putting *im-*, meaning "not," in front of the following words to reverse their meaning:

partial	perfect
modest	patient
moderate	

What is a *turbid* lake?

Syllabification for correct spelling

---

im-per-turb-a-ble

14 aerophobia /air o fo bee uh /âr' ə fō' bē ə

Aerophobia means a fear or at least strong dislike of flying. It describes a person who is reluctant to or will not get into an airplane (originally spelled *aeroplane*).

Another old meaning of *aerophobia* is fear or dislike of drafts or fresh air.

aeronautics – the science that deals with the operation of aircraft or, in fact, just about anything to do with airplanes. The root *nautics* comes from *nautical,* meaning "ship," and got incorporated into this word in the days when *aircraft* meant lighter-than-air "ships" (such as balloons and blimps) that were sailed through the air.

Root *aero* means simply "air."

The root *phobia* in *aerophobia* means "fear" or "strong dislike." The degree can vary from simply avoiding to outright panic with severe bodily reaction such as paralysis or increased heart rate.

Here are a couple of other phobias:

acrophobia (fear of heights) **claustrophobia** (fear of enclosed spaces)

bibliophobia (fear of books) **cynophobia** (fear of dogs)

bathophobia (fear of depths, not fear of baths)

There is a big list of *phobias* in Appendix D.

Any *phobia* can also be a *philia,* so it can be a "love of" rather than a "fear of." For example, *cynophilia* is a love of dogs.

Activities

Do you know any other *phobias*?
What could you call someone who doesn't like open windows?
How many syllables are there in *aerophobia*?
What would you call someone who really loves dogs?

Syllabification for correct spelling

_____

aer-o-pho-bi-a

Magnanimous means having a lofty, courageous spirit. It suggests an attitude of nobility, generosity, and being above pettiness and meanness: "The team was *magnanimous* after it lost the game, showing great friendship toward the victors." "The big company that bought out the smaller company was *magnanimous* toward the new employees and let them all keep their jobs." Both the team and the company showed great *magnanimity* /mag nan im i tee/.

Root
magna means "great"; *animus* means "spirit" or "alive."

magna cum laude – with highest praise; an honor that the best students are given at graduation.

magna carta (also spelled *magna charta*) – the famous English civil rights document that really is a "great charter."

charter – a written contract or instrument establishing something, for example, a *charter* school.

magnate – a big-time operator in an industry, such as a tobacco or real estate *magnate*.

animated – lifelike or full of life. The characters in *animated* cartoons are lifelike; they have sound and motion. An *animated* conversation is lively or spirited.

animal – a living creature of the biological classification *Animalia*.

pusillanimous – lacking in courage or resolution; mean-spirited and timid. (*pusil-* = very small)

Activities

Describe a situation in which someone was *magnanimous*.

What U.S. document is similar to the English *Magna Carta*?

A person who runs the biggest cheese factory in your area could be called a _____.

Is *pusillanimous* the opposite of *magnanimous*?

Syllabification for correct spelling

_____

mag-nan-i-mous

16 zealot /zell utt   /zel' ət

A *zealot* is somebody with too much *zeal*. *Zeal* is a nice word for "a lot of enthusiasm or eagerness." But calling somebody a *zealot* is not polite. The word *zealot* is frequently used in a religious sense, as in *religious zealot*. In fact, the association is so common that the whole phrase *religious zealot* need not be applied to someone's religious enthusiasm. So the word might be used to mean that a person is a little crazy, with too strong or too narrow religious beliefs, but the person probably just thinks of himself as being very devoted.

Fewer words begin with *Z* than with any other letter except *X*.

And most of the Z words tend not to be in families or to have a root that is found in other words. For example:

zenith /zee nith/ – the summit or highest point. *Zenith* may be used to refer to the highest point on a mountain, or to the highest point in someone's career. But *zenith* also has a more technical meaning: it is the point directly overhead when you are looking at the sky. Incidentally, *zenith* is one of the relatively few words we have gotten from Arabic.

zero – another Arabic word, the mathematical symbol for nothing, 0. Discovering the zero was a huge advance in mathematics over the Roman numeral system (CXVIII=118).

zephyr – a light breeze; from the Roman god *Zephyrus,* the god of the west wind.

Activities

Look in your dictionary and see how big the Z section is compared to other letter sections.

Would you call a friend a *zealot*?

Would a *zephyr* blow your hat off?

Identify two important words that come from Arabic.

> **Syllabification for correct spelling**
> _____
> **zeal-ot**

Bibliophobia is a fear or strong dislike of books. Maybe you know some students like that.

In ancient Greece and Rome, books were written on papyrus and papyrus was shipped from the Phoenician port of *Byblos*, in the area we today call Lebanon. Here are some other *biblio*- words:

Root
biblio means "books." It has an interesting history.

bibliography – a list of books or articles. (-*graph* = write)

bibliomania – an extreme interest in books, especially in owning them. (-*mania* = madness)

biblioklept – a book stealer. *klept*- means stealing and is used in *kleptomania* (meaning "a madness for stealing").

bibliophile – a person who loves books and probably collects them and reads all the time. (-*phile* = love)

bibliophage – someone who reads a lot of books, or literally eats them. -*phage* means to eat, so a *bibliophage* may literally be a "bookworm."

-*phage* is frequently used in biology, as in:

bacteriophage – a type of cell that eats or destroys bacteria.

Activities

Are *bibliophobia* and *bibliomania* antonyms?

Could a person who won't return a borrowed book be called a *biblioklept*?

Look up Phoenicia on a map (today it is called Syria and Lebanon).

Are *bibliophile* and *bibliomania* synonyms?

Syllabification for correct spelling
___
bib-li-o-pho-bi-a

Impede means to slow something down or to get in the way of progress: "Traffic signals *impede* your progress across town." (The prefix *im-* is the same as the prefix *in-*; both mean "in.") So, to *impede* means literally to put your foot in the works.

expedite – the opposite of *impede*. The prefix *ex-* means "out." To *expedite* something means to get going faster or "get your foot out."

impedimenta – things that slow you down, such as carrying too many bags when you are in a hurry to catch a plane. *Impedimenta* is a noun while *impede* is a verb.

Root
ped means "foot."

impediment – a singular noun that means the same thing as *impedimenta,* which is plural and a bit more formal. It is also correct, however, to use the plural *impediments*: "A lisp is a speech *impediment*."

expedition – originally meant "travel on foot" but nowadays can mean any kind of travel, but particularly with a specific purpose: "They set out on an *expedition* to find the lost dog."

pedal – a place for your foot that is attached to a lever.

pedometer – a measuring instrument that gives an estimate of distance walked. (*-meter* = measure)

The root *ped* can also be used to count:

biped – two-footed creature, such as a human

quadruped – four-footed creature, such as a dog

centipede – an insect with supposedly a hundred feet

millipede – an insect with supposedly a thousand feet

Activities

Where have you seen something impede progress?

If you wanted to measure how far you walked you would use a _____.

Name some other *quadrupeds*.

Has anybody really counted the feet on a *millipede*?

Syllabification for correct spelling
_____
im-pede

19 bursar /bur sar /bûr' sər

A *bursar* is a treasurer or the person who holds the money in an organization, such as a college or a religious organization.

The suffix *-ar* means "a person who," so a *bursar* is a person who holds the purse. The suffix *-ar* is used in many common words, such as *liar* and *beggar*.

bursa – an English word used in medicine, meaning a *sac* or fluid-filled pouch that may be in or near a joint. Note the spelling of *sac. Sac* and *suck* sound the same and have similar meanings, but *sack* is used in the grocery store and *sac* is used in the doctor's office.

Root
burs comes from the Latin *bursa,* meaning "purse."

bursitis – a condition in which the bursa get inflamed. The suffix *-itus,* meaning "inflamed," is used in a lot of other words, such as *arthritis*, which involves inflammation of the joints, and *tendonitus,* which involves inflammation of the tendons.

disburse – to pay out money, especially public funds; can also mean to distribute anything of value, such as property. (*dis-* = from, as in "from the purse")

disbursement – the actual payment; the money or item disbursed.

reimburse – to pay back, perhaps for something stolen or damaged; to repay; to make restoration for a payment delayed. (*re-* = back)

Activities

If you damage an insured car, the insurance company will _____ you for the damages.

In a college, who holds the money and pays the bills?

What is a *disbursement*?

In a grocery store they put the groceries in a _____ (spell it correctly).

Syllabification for correct spelling
_____
bur-sar

20 antidote /an ti doht /an' ti dōt'/

An *antidote* is something given to counteract a poison or something injurious: "If you are struck by a rattlesnake you had better get an *antidote*." "An aspirin is a mild *antidote* for a headache."

So an *antidote* works against the dose or poison you have received.

dose – a portion or measured amount given: "The doctor prescribed a *dose* of *antibiotics* to kill off the little microbes causing your illness." A *dose* can also mean an action: "He had a *dose* of bad luck."

Root
anti means "against"; *dote* means "give."

overdose – a dose that is too large and could make you worse. Or to say it another way, you hope the *dosage* is correct.

doting – being overly fond and giving: "The grandparents were *doting* over the new baby." "They should not dote too much."

Don't confuse *antidote* /an ti' doht/ with *anecdote* /an ek' doht/, which is a short, amusing, or personal story: "Dad often tells *anecdotes* about his boyhood days."

Activities

A lot of words begin with *anti-*; name some of them.

A main job for a pharmacist is to give you the correct _____.

If you are poisoned, do you want an *anecdote*?

Does the label on a medicine bottle tell you the *dosage*?

Syllabification for correct spelling
_____
an-ti-dote

21 tantalize /tan tuh lize   /tan' tl īz'

The word *tantalize* comes from an old Greek myth about a bad king who, for his sins, was condemned to stand in water up to his chin. But whenever he got thirsty and tried to drink the water, it went away. When he was hungry and went to a fruit tree and tried to pick a piece, the branches moved away. Hence the word *tantalize* means to "tease" or "torment" by presenting something desired and then keeping it just out of reach: "She *tantalized* her dog by holding a bone just out of its reach." "Miners were *tantalized* into digging when they found tiny flecks of gold, but the digging didn't yield any significant amounts."

Root
tant means "as much as."

But this root really isn't very helpful. Only a few words use it.

tantamount – having an equivalent or similar amount or value: "Passing the GED is *tantamount* to high school graduation." The root *amount* means "amount"—too easy.

tantalum – a basic metallic element. *Tantalum* does not react or corrode easily and is used for metallic parts put into the human body: "His hip replacement had *tantalum* in it."

Activities

Do you know a situation in which someone was *tantalized*?

What would you like a knee replacement to be made of?

Identify some other situations that are *tantamount* to each other.

Which of these two words—*tantalize* or *tantamount*—is closer to *tease*?

Syllabification for correct spelling

_____

tan-ta-lize

Pathetic means a feeling of pity, sympathy, tenderness, or sorrow toward a person or situation: "Their home was not just bad, it was *pathetic*." "The cat didn't drown but it certainly looked *pathetic*."

sympathy – the prefix *sym-* means "with," so if you extend *sympathy* to somebody you are "feeling with" them.

Root
path comes from Greek and means "feeling" or "sensitive."

apathy – the prefix *a-* sometimes means "without," so *apathy* means "without feeling," but it can also mean you can't get going or have no feeling for something.

antipathy – the prefix *anti-* means against, opposite, or opposed, so *antipathy* is almost the opposite of *sympathy*. In fact, *antipathy* can mean a strong dislike or direct opposite.

sociopath – a person who has no feeling for society. Frequently, *sociopaths* are people who commit crimes and get put in prison.

Activities

What are some other *pathetic* situations or persons?

If you don't like football you have *apathy,* but if you hate it you have _____.

An ax murderer is almost certainly a _____.

Is a member of a gang a *sociopath*?

Syllabification for correct spelling
_____
pa-thet-ic

The word *ingratiate* means "to seek favor" or "to present in a pleasing manner": "The new employee tried to *ingratiate* himself with the boss by working hard."

So *ingratiate* means "to seek to please." But watch out for the prefix *in-*, which in *ingratiate* means "in" and in *ingratitude* means "not."

Root
grat means "pleasing" or "grace."

grateful – pleased or appreciative, perhaps even indebted.

ungrateful – the opposite of grateful; unthankful or unappreciative.

gratitude – thankfulness or appreciation.

ingratitude – the opposite of gratitude.

gratuity /gra too i tee/ – a tip or honorarium—usually money.

gratis – free; you don't have to pay.

congratulate – to compliment or wish well.

Activities

How can you *ingratiate* yourself with your teacher?

Would you buy a ticket that said *gratis* on it?

How do you pronounce the third syllable of *ingratiate*?

A kid who doesn't say thank-you shows _____.

Syllabification for correct spelling

_____

in-gra-ti-ate

24 oblique /oh bleek /ə blēk'

Oblique is an interesting word because it is applied in so many areas. First, the simple definition is "to slant in direction or position." Hence the object is neither straightforward nor perpendicular. *Oblique* may refer to a line that goes in an odd direction, or it might apply to a remark that refers to something not directly related to the topic: "The road takes off at an *oblique* angle." "I couldn't figure out his *oblique* suggestion."

Both of these meanings connote a "bend." *Oblique* is used in a number of fields, such as:

Root
liquis comes from Latin and means "to turn aside" or "elbow."

the military – The soldiers marched *obliquely,* at 45 degrees to the original line of troops.

biology – Muscles situated *obliquely* are attached to one end of a bone.

astronomy – The axis of an *oblique* sphere is at an angle to the observer's sphere. The earth's axis is oblique to the plane of annual rotation.

geology – An *oblique* fault is at an angle to the strike (general slope of the layers).

geometry – An *oblique* triangle is any triangle other than a right triangle. (There are no right angles in the triangle.)

architecture – An *oblique* arch is not set at a right angle to a wall.

Activities

Point out things set at an *oblique* angle in any room.

Make an *oblique* remark about your government.

If one end of an *oblique* muscle is attached to a bone, to what is the other end attached?

What are some *oblique* roads in your area?

Syllabification for correct spelling

_____

o-blique

A *necropolis* is "a city of the dead." Hence it is a high-class word for a cemetery, particularly a large and fancy cemetery. It can also refer to an ancient city where nobody lives anymore, or a prehistoric burial place.

necrophobia – an abnormal fear of dying. (*-phobia* = fear)

necrology – a list of persons who have died. (*-logy* = study of)

necrobiosis – the death of living tissue. (*bio* = life; *sis* = process or action)

necrolatry – worship of the dead. (*-latry* = worship)

Incidentally, if you respect a culture's necrolatry, you call it their *religion;* but if you wish to disparage their necrolatry or put it down, you call it a *superstition.*

The *-polis* in *necropolis* means "city," which is seen in some other common words, such as:

politician – elected government official; person of the city. (*-ian* = person)

cosmopolitan – related to the city or cities (*cosmo-* = universe): "She is very *cosmopolitan*" means she is of the city or very sophisticated.

Root
necro means "dead."

Activities

People who won't even go near a cemetery have _____.

Some organizations keep a list of dead members called a _____.

Ancestor worship is also called _____.

The pyramids in Egypt are part of a _____.

Syllabification for correct spelling
_____
ne-crop-o-lis

26 decibel /des ih bull /des' ə bel'

A *decibel* is a unit of hearing. In fact, it is the smallest change in *loudness* that a human can detect. Scientists call this change the *jnd*, for just noticeable difference. Decibels range from 1, for the faintest sound you can hear, to 130, which is so loud it is sure to damage your hearing quickly. Very loud amplified music can slowly damage your hearing permanently.

Root
dec means "ten."

decagon – a ten-sided and ten-angled plane figure.

decimeter – one tenth of a meter in length.

December – the tenth month in the old Julian calendar.

decathlon – an athletic contest with ten events.

decade – ten years.

decagon – a ten-angled figure.

The unit *-bel* was named for Alexander Graham Bell, inventor of the telephone.

Activities

Draw a line 2 *decimeters* long.

The building was shaped like a _____; it was almost round.

The month of _____ is now our twelfth month.

If a sound has too many _____ it is painful.

Syllabification for correct spelling
_____
dec-i-bel

27 genocide /gen o side /jen' ə sīd'

Genocide is an attempt to kill off a whole race or political or cultural group. The classic example was when Hitler tried to kill off all Jews. He did kill millions, but not all. *Genocide* is still going on, most recently in Africa.

gender – classification of sex differences; male or female.

general – a whole race or class of things; not detailed (adj.): "*Generally* he is a good kid."

General – officer in charge of a whole army (noun).

generation – a group born at about the same time.

insecticide – a substance that kills insects.

suicide – the killing of oneself.

Root
gen comes from Greek and means "race" or "kind."

Appendix D contains a list of roots that can be combined with *-cide*.

Suffix
-cide means "killing."

Activities

To call someone a boy or girl is to classify that person by _____.

Trying to kill a whole race, as happened in Germany and is happening in Africa, is _____.

A high-ranking army officer is a _____.

In _____, I'm feeling fine.

Syllabification for correct spelling
_____
gen-o-cide

28 feng shui /feng shway /feng shuay

Feng shui is the ancient Chinese practice of harmonizing buildings, rooms, and gardens with nature. For example, buildings facing south are thought to have better *chi* (energy). At least they might have better light if they are in the northern hemisphere. Good chi can bring good fortune, which often means health and prosperity.

Feng shui is related to the three-thousand-year-old philosophy of Taoism. *Tao* means "the way" or behavior that is in harmony with nature. *Feng* means "wind" and *shui* means "water." So *feng shui* literally means "wind and water," two of nature's basic forces. *Feng shui* is really a compound word with a slightly different meaning from the separate words.

Here are a few other Chinese words that are common in English:

chow – In English *chow* is slang for "food," but in Peking it means "meat dumpling."

chow mein – In China, *mein* means "flour" or "dough." In the United States, *chow mein* often means a stew served with fried noodles.

kowtow – In China, *kowtow* means to kneel and touch your forehead to the ground as an act of deep respect or worship. In the United States, it means to submit to an authority, maybe a little too much.

gung ho – In China, *gung ho* means to work together cooperatively. In the United States, it means "enthusiastic," "zealous," or "to work hard."

Activities

How can a house have good *chi*?

What is the basic idea of *Tao*?

Is *kowtow* derogatory in China?

How could you describe an enthusiastic worker?

> **Syllabification for correct spelling**
> _____
> **feng shui**

At a graduation the *salutatorian* is the graduate with the second highest rank or grade score. It is his or her job to give a *salute*, which is a welcome, greeting, honoring, or wish for good health. It comes from the name of the Roman goddess of health, Salus.

salutatory – the speech the *salutatorian* gives to the graduates.

Root
salu means "health."

salute – in the military, a formal greeting such as raising a hand to the forehead or tipping one's hat; also the firing of rifles or cannons at a funeral or welcoming ceremony.

salutation – the opening greeting of a letter, such as "Dear John."

salubrious – promoting good health: "Mountain air is *salubrious*."

salvation – to be removed from danger: "Winning the lottery was his *salvation*."

valedictorian – the graduate whose job at the end of the graduation ceremony is to say farewell. As the student with the highest grades, he or she gets the last word. Note that *valid* means "strong or well grounded" and *dict* refers to "speech," so the *valedictorian* had better give a strong speech.

Activities

Pronounce all six syllables in *salutatorian*.

What is the best student called?

What does the *salutatorian* give?

Name something *salubrious*.

Syllabification for correct spelling
—————————
sa-lu-ta-to-ri-an

30 emancipate /ee man suh payt /i man' sə pāt'

President Lincoln was in favor of *emancipating* the slaves. That meant setting them free. They would no longer be in bondage or owned by someone else. He was an *emancipator*.

Emancipate can also apply to children. It is a legal term. A court can *emancipate* a child from his or her parent's authority. It does not happen often and is used only in special circumstances.

The hands of someone who is *emancipated* are figuratively or literally set free and the person is no longer bound.

Many of the words that contain *-man* are related to "handle."

Root
man means "hand." The prefix *e-* means "out" or "not."

manager – someone who is in charge of or handles a situation or organization.

management – a collection of managers.

unmanageable – cannot be managed.

manufacture – originally, to make something by hand.

manual labor – labor that uses the hands.

manuscript – originally, any handwritten document. Today, *manuscript* means an original or unpublished copy of a book or play. *Manuscript* also means a type of handwriting in which the letters are separated, not connected. (*-script* = writing)

Activities

To free slaves is to _____ them.

Manual labor is work
    using _____.

The prefix *e-* in *emancipate*
    means _____.

Where in the world are some people not *emancipated* today?

Syllabification for correct spelling

_____
e-man-ci-pate

31 indoctrinate /in dok truh nate /in dok' trə nāt'

Indoctrinate has both a good and a bad meaning. At worst it means to "brainwash" or to fill another person's mind with a narrow belief that you do not like. It also implies not telling both sides of an issue, such as both its good and its bad aspects. A more positive use of *indoctrinate* is to "teach" or "educate." All cultures *indoctrinate* their youth into certain beliefs or values; in the United States, democracy is a belief that is *indoctrinated*.

Root
doc comes from the Latin *docere,* which means "to teach."

doctor – historically, someone with enough knowledge to teach. Universities grant doctoral degrees, such as a PhD, which means *doctor* of philosophy, and MD, which means *doctor* of medicine. Not all PhDs and MDs teach, so the degree now represents mastering a body of knowledge in a certain field.

docent – someone who guides you around a museum and teaches you about the exhibits.

doctrine – something taught as an official principle or belief, such as a legal or religious *doctrine*.

doctrinaire – holding a view of something perhaps a bit too narrowly or impractically.

docile – describes a person or an animal who can be taught and is not rebellious. More widely used to mean "calm."

Activities

Would you like to be *indoctrinated* about ballet?

Tell your *doctor* he is really a teacher.

Could you call your teacher a *docent*?

What is the opposite of *docile*?

Syllabification for correct spelling

———————

in-doc-tri-nate

You have certainly heard of the Declaration of Independence. What is a *declaration*? It is a public statement, often formal. It is also a slang expression of surprise, as in "Well, I declare!" In court a *declaratio*n is the opening statement or complaint of the plaintiff (the person bringing the problem to court). Corporations *declare a dividend,* which is a sum of money to be divided between the company's stockholders. Governments *declare* peace to end a war formally and officially.

Root

clar comes from Latin and means "clear."

clear – transparent, as in "*clear* glass," or easily understood, as in "Did I make that *clear*?"

clarify – to make something clear: "You can *clarify* a liquid by straining out all the little solid bits; you can *clarify* an idea by making it more understandable."

claret – a clear red wine, originally from France; a medium red color, lighter than crimson.

clarion – a trumpet from the Middle Ages, noted for its clear notes; in modern times, a horn or an organ.

clarinet – reed instrument popular in jazz bands and school bands; a modification of the *clarion*. (suffix *-et* = small)

Activities

Can you think of any other *declarations*?

What is the opposite of *declaring* peace?

Is it possible to *clarify* soup?

See if your music teacher knows the origin of the word *clarinet*.

Syllabification for correct spelling

dec-la-ra-tion

33 gullible /gull ih bull/ gul ə bəl

Somebody who is *gullible* is easily cheated, easily deceived, or easily duped: "She got a bad insurance policy because she was so *gullible*."

gullet – synonym for "throat," used particularly for humans and birds. Technically the *gullet* is the *esophagus,* or the passage through which food passes on the way to the stomach. Both food or an idea that you can't quite swallow might "stick in your *gullet*."

Root
gul, from Middle English or Old French, means "throat."

seagulls – a common class of birds. Members of the Audubon Society try never to use the term *seagull*. They do sometimes use *gull* (noun), but they prefer a more precise classification, such as "California gull" or "black-headed gull."

gull (verb) – to cheat or dupe: "He *gulled* the whole crowd with his fast talk." *Gull* may also be applied to the person being cheated: "He found a *gull* at the carnival." In this case, a *gull* is a person who will swallow anything.

gully (also correctly spelled *gulley*) – a miniature valley or gorge caused by running water. Could also be called a *gulch*.

Activities

Could a person who is *gullible* get cheated?

Tell about a time when you were a *gull*.

Are there any *gullies* in your neighborhood?

Where have you seen *gulls*?

Syllabification for correct spelling

_____

gul-li-ble

Someone who is *gregarious* likes to be around people, particularly his friends or people like himself. You might call him a "party animal," but at the least he doesn't like to be alone. A *gregarious* person likes to be with the herd. Many animals and birds are *gregarious,* and so are some wild plants and insects.

Root
greg comes from Latin and means "herd" or "flock."

egregious – If a "party animal" does something really bad, he is kicked out of the herd for his behavior. The prefix *e-* means "out."*Egregious* can also apply to anything done or spoken in extremely bad taste.

congregate – forming a group of people or animals (*con-* = with)

congregation – a group of people gathered in a church or some other formal occasion.

aggregation – any group of people, animals, or things. (*ag-* = to)

segregation – the setting apart or isolation of a small group or an individual; the rules or customs of keeping people or things separated from other groups.

desegregation – the system of canceling the rules or customs of segregation when people or objects are allowed back together. (*de-* = from)

Activities

Describe a friend who is *gregarious.*

Give an example of *egregious* behavior.

To whom or what do *segregation* laws apply?

A collection of things can be called a(n) _____.

Syllabification for correct spelling
_____
gre-gar-i-ous

A *preamble* is the introductory part of a document or book. It is also used for laws or legal documents; for example, the *Preamble* to the U.S. Constitution tells why the Constitution was written. It is a short philosophical statement that appears before the *articles*, which specify how the government is to be established. Article 1 states, "All *legislative* [law-making] powers shall be vested in a congress."

Root
amble means "to walk"; *pre-* means "before."

A similar word is *preface*, usually brief notes written by the author and placed at the front of a book. Another similar word is *introduction*, which can be longer and written by either the author or somebody else. *Introduction* is also used to refer to somebody *introducing* a speaker or two strangers.

So a *preamble* is something that "comes before."

circumambulate – to walk around (*curcum-* = circle). Hence, *circumambulate* can literally mean to walk around something or to talk all around the main point.

ambulatory – able to walk; often used to describe recovering sick people who are now walking.

amble – to walk slowly or leisurely.

ambiguous – wandering or uncertain, as in speech or writing; understandable in two or more ways.

Activities

Read the *Preamble* to the U.S. Constitution—it's very short.

Look at several books and see if they have a *preface* or an *introduction*.

A bad speech can be _____.

In India, some people pray by walking around a temple. They are _____ing.

Syllabification for correct spelling

_____
pre-am-ble

A *plutocracy* is a government run by the wealthy, the big-money class. The big-money people could be called *plutocrats* (wealthy rulers). In the 1800s, John D. Rockefeller was called a plutocrat because he was very wealthy from oil extracted in Ohio and refined in New Jersey. He had some control over those states' governments and got favorable concessions. He later gave much money to charity, but his children inherited much wealth in banking and real estate in New York (Rockefeller Center).

The word is related to Pluto, the Greek god of the underworld. *Underworld* in this case means not hell or crime, but where mineral wealth comes from, such as gold and gem mines. Rockefeller probably had some *plutogogues* around; these are people who favor wealthy persons and give them good publicity.

Root
pluto means "wealth."
cracy means "rule."

democracy – rule by all the people. (*demo-* = people)

oligarchy – rule by just a few people. (*olig-* = few)

autocracy – rule by just one person. (*auto-* = self)

monarchy – rule by a monarch, a king or queen. (*mono-* = single)

theocracy – rule by a priestly or religious class. (*theo-* = god)

kleptocracy – rule by thieves or for personal gain. (*klept-* = steal)

bureaucracy – rule by office employees. (*bureau* = office)

bureaucrat – a person who works in a government bureau.

Activities

What kind of rule would you prefer?

What kind of rule would you hate the most?

Who was *Pluto*?

Who was John D. Rockefeller?

Syllabification for correct spelling
_____
plu-toc-ra-cy

Photosynthesis is the combining of chemical elements using light. The most common example is in living plants, where carbon dioxide forms carbohydrates using sunlight and water. This process causes the plants to grow and puts fresh oxygen into the air. This is, incidentally, a major ecological reason we need large masses of plants, such as forests, over much of the earth.

The root *syn-* in *photosynthesis* means "together" or "together with," and the root *-thesis* means "laying down a position or proposition." So, in *photosynthesis,* a number of elements are put together. More common uses of the word *thesis* are to refer to a paper required for an academic degree or to a formal position statement.

Root
photo comes from Greek and means "light."

photography – a process that uses light to make a picture by projecting an image onto chemicals.

photosensitive – sensitive to light. For example, a coating of chemicals on film changes when light is applied. Plants, people's skin, and photocells also are *photosensitive.*

photogenic – looks good in pictures. The root *gen* means "born," so perhaps the *photogenic* girl is born that way.

Activities

If you wanted to compliment your girlfriend on how she appears in a photograph, you could say that she is very _____.

Most plants use _____ to grow.

Do modern (digital) cameras use *photosynthesis*?

Are most writing assignments given to students in school called a *thesis*?

Syllabification for correct spelling

_____

pho-to-syn-the-sis

Corpulent means having a large, bulky body. You might also say the person is *fat,* or if you are kinder, you might say the person is big-boned or husky. And if you want to hide behind a big word, the person is *obese* /oh beess/. You could say the person is *stout, fleshy, massive,* or just *large.* These are all synonyms for *corpulent.*

corpse /korps/ – dead body.

corps /kor/ – a group of people, as in Marine *Corps.*

Root
corp means "body."

corporation – a body of persons associated for some purpose. Commonly means a business that is treated under the law as a person so that it can conduct business, such as owning property or being sued. A city government is also usually a *corporation.*

unincorporated – not a corporation. Frequently refers to an area that is not included in a city or to a business that is not a corporation.

corpuscle – any tiny particle but usually refers to a living cell, such as a red blood cell, muscle cell, or a plant leaf cell.

corporeal – of the physical body; not spiritual.

corporal – same pronunciation and meaning as corporeal; also a non-commissioned army officer.

corporal punishment – hitting or causing pain.

Activities

Is your body made up of *corpuscles*?

Can a dog be *corpulent*?

Do you live in an *incorporated* area?

What is a nice way to describe a fat person?

Syllabification for correct spelling
_____
cor-pu-lent

38

39 benevolent /beh nev uh lent / bə nev' ə lənt

Benevolent is an adjective used to describe a person who is kind and generous, who promotes the happiness and prosperity of other people. It could also apply to organizations that do likewise: "The *benevolent* Gates Foundation gives money and organizational skills to help stamp out AIDS in Africa."

benefactor – a person who is *benevolent* (*factor* = "doer"): "Bill and Melinda Gates are *benefactors*."

Prefix *bene*- means simply "good" or "well."

benefit – something that aids or promotes something good. For example, a *benefit* might be a show to raise money for the handicapped. You could also *benefit* from investing your money wisely.

beneficial – something that is good: "Rain is *beneficial* for the corn crop."

benign – good or well: "The tumor was *benign;* there was no sign of cancer."

benediction – good words or a blessing: "The priest gave a short *benediction* at the end of the wedding ceremony."

beneficiary – the person or organization who receives a benefit. For example, the *beneficiary* of a life insurance policy is the person who gets the money when the insured person dies.

Activities

Have you ever been to a *benefit*?

Can you name any *benevolent* acts?

If you have a medical test, you want the results to be _____.

Who are your *benefactors*?

> **Syllabification for correct spelling**
> _____
> be-nev-o-lent

Orthodontics is a branch of dentistry that deals with irregularities in teeth. It can also be called teeth straightening. The specialized dentist who does this is an *orthodontist.*

The *ortho-* in *orthodontics* means "straight." Hence, the simple translation of *orthodontics* is "straight teeth."

dentist – a professional who treats diseases of the teeth.

exodontia – the extraction of teeth. An *exodontist* pulls teeth.

Root
dont is a variation of *dent,* which means "tooth."

dandelion – French for "dent de lion," meaning "teeth of a lion." A *dandelion* is a common yellow flower seen growing in some lawns; it has many petals, or teeth.

orthopedist – historically, a doctor who treated children, helping them to grow straight. Today an *orthopedic* physician is concerned with muscles and the skeleton. A football player or senior citizen with bad knees goes to an *orthopedic* doctor. *Ped-* means "child," so a doctor who now specializes in treating children is called a *pediatrician.*

orthodox – the straight and strict following of a belief. The root *dox* means "belief" or "opinion."

Activities

Do you know someone who has had *orthodontia*?

What does *ortho* mean?

What is another word for *false teeth*?

What kinds of organizations are frequently called *orthodox*?

Syllabification for correct spelling
_____
or-tho-don-tics

41 edict /ee dikt /ē' dikt

An *edict* is a public notice put out by an authority, such as a government or a religious authority. It is something like a law or an official pronouncement made by a king, religious leader, or dictator. Congress votes to make laws; kings pronounce *edicts*.

verdict – the judgment of a judge or jury about the innocence of a person charged with a crime or about which side is right in a civil case. Because court cases often hang on which person is telling the truth, *verdict* literally means "true saying."

Root
dict means "speak."

vindicate – to set free or tell which side is right. The verdict vindicated the accused criminal, or settled a suit about money.

predict – to tell what will happen in the future (*pre-* = before)

contradict – to speak against or bring out the opposite (*contra-* = opposite)

dictation – one person speaks while another person writes it down

Activities

If you are charged with a crime, you would like to be _____.

Can you argue with an *edict*?

Juries give a _____.

Give some examples of ideas or things that *contradict* each other.

Syllabification for correct spelling
_____
e-dict

42 countermand /koun ter mand /koun' tər mand'

To *countermand* is to stop or change a command or an order. It is a fancy way of saying "cancel" or "do the opposite": "The sergeant *countermanded* the first order." (*counter-* = against)

command – an official order or strong request: "The general issued a *command*." (*com-* = with)

commander – the person who gives the orders. Also the rank of a military officer.

Root
mand means "to order" or "to enjoin."

demand – a formal requirement, such as a court order, or strong request: "I *demand* that you stop it!" *Demand* can also indicate a need: "There is a *demand* for more cell phones."

mandate – an order or authorization: "The election gave the president a *mandate* for change."

mandatory – compulsory or required: "A course in English is *mandatory*."

remand – to send back: "The judge *remanded* the prisoner to jail." (*re-* = back)

Activities

Can you name a product for which there is a *demand*?

What law would you like to see *countermanded*?

If you were a mayor, what would you *mandate*?

If you wanted to change a book order, you would _____.

Syllabification for correct spelling
_____
coun-ter-mand

43 cognitive /kog ni tiv   /kog' ni tiv

Cognitive means "learning" or "thinking." A *cognitive* experience is usually a learning experience. Hopefully you have a lot of *cognitive* experiences in school.

recognize – to know or remember something or somebody: "It's very dark if you can't *recognize* your best friend." The prefix *re-* means "back," so *recognizing* involves *recall* of some past learning.

cognizant – aware: "She wasn't *cognizant* of what was about to happen."

cognoscente /kon yu shen' tee/ – a person who knows a lot about a particular field of knowledge, usually the arts or literature: "A *cognoscente* judged the picture to be an original." The plural of *cognoscente* is **cognoscenti** /kon yu shen' tee/: "The two *cognoscenti* judged the picture differently."

Root

cogn means "to learn" or "to know."

precognition – knowing beforehand. In other words, *clairvoyance* or *mental telepathy*. *Precognition* could be just a hunch or a feeling that something is going to happen: "Fortune-tellers and prophets supposedly have *precognition* so they can tell you what will happen in the future."

cognate – a word that is similar in meaning, sound, and spelling to a word in another language. The Spanish word *junio* is a cognate of the English word *June*.

Activities

Name at least one *cognitive* experience you have had in school.

What are you *cognizant* of right now?

What are two or more *cognoscente* called?

Do you know any other *cognates* in Spanish and English?

Syllabification for correct spelling

_____

cog-ni-tive

Supervene means "to come after" or "in addition." "The panel discussion *supervened* the main address." "We don't want any more ideas to *supervene*."

convene – to call a group of persons together.

> **convention** – an assembly of persons. (*con-* = with)

> **conventional** – ordinary or traditional.

> **adventure** – to venture or go forth; current meaning encompasses an element of danger or risk. (*ad-* = to)

> **intervene** – to come between: "Don't *intervene* in another family's argument." (*inter-* = between)

> **revenue** – often money that comes back from an investment or business; also, tax money that comes back to the government. (*re-* = back)

Root
super means "over" or "in addition to"; *ven* means "come."

Activities

When have you seen something *supervene*?

Is the way you dress *conventional*?

Have you ever *intervened* in a discussion?

What is the source of *revenue* for your school?

> **Syllabification for correct spelling**
> _____
> su-per-vene

45 kaleidoscope /ka lie duh scope   /kə lī' də skōp'

A *kaleidoscope*, as you probably know, is a child's toy or an adult amusement instrument that you look through to see an interesting color pattern. When you rotate the *kaleidoscope*, the pattern changes through an infinite number of variations.

The *kaleidoscope* works by having a number of fragments of colored glass between two sheets of glass that tumble into different arrangements when the *kaleidoscope* is turned. These arrangements are then reflected in several mirrors and passed to your eye through light.

Kaleidoscope can also mean a jumble of colorful things: "The circus ring was a *kaleidoscope* of color." The Greek word *kalos* means "beautiful." It is the beginning part of *California*.

Root
scope means "to view."

telescope – an instrument for viewing distant objects (*tele-* = far)

microscope – an instrument for viewing small objects (*micro-* = small)

stethoscope – an instrument for listening to faint or soft sounds. Your doctor puts his *stethoscope* to your chest to hear your heart beat and your lungs work. (*steth-* = chest)

horoscope – a diagram showing the positions of planets; used by astrologers to predict favorable times for events. (*horo-* = hour)

Activities

Describe a pattern you might see in a *kaleidoscope*.

What does *scope* mean?

What kind of problems can a *stethoscope* reveal?

Have you seen *horoscope* predictions in your newspaper?

Syllabification for correct spelling
_____
ka-lei-do-scope

46 tacit /tass it   /tas' it

Tacit means "silent." A *tacit* agreement between businesspeople means that it is understood but not spoken and certainly not written: "The gas stations had a *tacit* agreement to raise prices on the same day."

taciturn – describes people who are retiring and uncommunicative; they are tacit, or silent, most of the time.

reticent – inclined to keep silent, uncommunicative.

reserved – holds back emotions.

Root
tacit means "silent."

laconic – uses few words in speaking or writing; brief. "The staff asked the president of the company why she didn't answer questions more completely and give better explanations or longer orders. She replied, 'Why?'"

dour – silent, gloomy, ill-tempered, suspicious of strangers; rhymes with "sour."

acquiescent – complying tacitly (silently), accepting one's fate without complaining, passively.

Activities

An old codger who hates kids is _____.

Do teachers give good grades to *laconic* writers?

Would a *reserved* girl make a good cheerleader?

Can you tell whether an *acquiescent* employee likes his job?

Syllabification for correct spelling
_____
tac-it

47 decapitate /dee cap uh tate /di kap' i tāt'

Decapitate is a nice way of saying to cut off someone's head, or "to kill by beheading." Historically, it was a common way of killing, and unfortunately some of the "old days" are still with us.

capitol – a building in which a legislature (head law-making body) meets. The U.S. Congress meets in the *Capitol* building in Washington, D.C.

Root
capit means "head."

capital – the city of the seat (or head) of government. The federal *capital* of the United States is Washington, D.C., and each state has a *capital,* a city where the state's governor and legislature are located. So the *capitol* is always in the *capital.* See the difference a little *o* and *a* can make?

Capital also has many other uses. For example, a *capital crime* is one punishable by death; for a company, *capital* often means the money used to start up or continue business; for a politician, *capital* means the power or good-will usually gained by receiving a large number of votes; a *capital* in an alphabet is a large letter; and the British refer to a *capital fellow,* which means a man who is good or well liked.

When in doubt about whether to use the *a* spelling or the *o* spelling, use the *a* spelling. To help you remember the difference, recall that most *capitols* have a big round dome shaped like an *o.*

Capitol and *capital* are homophones.

Activities

When visiting Washington, D.C., be sure to head for the _____.

A murderer might be charged with a _____ crime.

This sentence starts with a _____ letter.

You might call your friend a _____ fellow.

Syllabification for correct spelling

_____

de-cap-i-tate

48 centennial /sen ten nee uhl /sen ten' ē əl

A *centennial* is a period of one hundred years. It can also be a commemoration or ceremonial remembrance of an event that happened a hundred years ago. (The root *-ennial* means "year," as in *biennial*, meaning two years.)

century – a hundred years. This is the 21st century AD (*anno domini*, or year of our Lord) or CE (Christian Era) because our calendar started in the year 0, at about the time of the birth of Jesus Christ, or CE (Common Era).

Root
cent
means "one hundred."

centigrade – one hundred gradations, but more commonly a system of measuring temperature used in Europe and much of the rest of the world as the metric system; 0 centigrade is the freezing point and 100 centigrade is the boiling point of water.

cent – a hundredth part of a basic monetary unit. In the United States it is a hundredth of a dollar. Don't confuse it with the homophone *scent*, which has to do with smelling.

centurion – a Roman army officer who commanded one hundred men.

centipede – an insect that supposedly has one hundred feet. (*ped* = foot)

centenarian – a person one hundred or more years old.

Activities

Do you know of any *centennial* commemorations?

Can a person 105 years old be called a *centenarian*?

If water freezes at 0 degrees *centigrade*, what is 100 degrees *centigrade*?

How many soldiers does a *centurion* order around?

Syllabification for correct spelling

cen-ten-ni-al

A *scriptorium* was a room where the monks of the Middle Ages (500 to 1500 AD) kept their *scripts*. The *scriptorium* also contained their *escriptories*, which were special writing desks. What did they write or copy? *Scripture*—the Holy Bible. Remember, Gutenberg didn't invent the printing press until the 1500s, so all books had to be copied using *manuscript*—that is, they were handwritten. (*manu-* = hand)

Things have changed a little since the Middle Ages, so today a *manuscript* usually refers to the original copy of a book or article. It is the writing before it is published.

Root
script **means "write."**

script – historically, handwriting of the book or a section of it being copied; now the written dialogue for a play or program.

postscript – the famous P.S., for *Post Script,* or additional material at the end of a letter. (*post-* = after)

prescription – a written order such as what your doctor writes to order medications; a written rule or law.

prescriptive – correct and in line with the rules. Using *prescriptive* grammar is using correct grammar when writing or speaking. (*pre-* = before)

proscribe – to prohibit or forbid something. Note again the difference made by one little letter. *Prescribe* tells you to do something and *proscribe* tells you not to do it. (*pro-* = before or for)

Activities

Where did the monks work?

Was 1200 AD in the Middle Ages?

What is a name for a desk used for *script* writing?

Can your doctor *proscribe* something?

Syllabification for correct spelling

scrip-to-ri-um

50 hydroponics /high dro pon iks /hī' drə pon' iks

Hydroponics is the growing of plants in water and not in earth. Well, that's not exactly true. The water must be a nutrient solution containing minerals and other elements that the plant needs. The plant must be supported somehow, such as by sand or gravel to hold the roots.

Prefix
hydro- means "water."

hydrophobia – means two things: first, it means a fear of water (*phobia-* = fear, in this and all the other phobias); second, it is also an informal word for the disease *rabies,* which occurs in dogs and other animals. Animals with this disease sometimes drool or appear to have water coming from the mouth.

hydrosphere – most of the water on Earth, including all the oceans, lakes, rivers, underground water, when moving and water vapor in the atmosphere.

hydrofoil – an underwater fin or a plate attached to struts that can lift the hull of a boat out of the water when moving so it can go faster.

hydrophyte – a plant that grows in water. (*phyte-* = plant) This is an example of many scientific terms that use *hydro-*.

Activities

Do plants growing in a *hydroponic* environment need sunlight?

What is another word for rabies?

Is a cloud part of the *hydrosphere*?

What do you call a plant that grows in water?

Syllabification for correct spelling
_____
hy-dro-pon-ics

51 audiometry /aw dee om eh tree /ô' dē om' i trē

Audiometry is testing done to see how well you hear or whether you are going deaf. It is done by a person called an *audiometrician* using an instrument called an *audiometer*. An *audiometrician* has studied *audiology,* the science of hearing disorders.

auditorium – a place where people gather to hear a speech or presentation of some sort. If the place is mainly for plays, it is called a theater. If it is mainly for music, it is called a hall.

Root
audio means "hearing."

audience – those who come to hear a performance or presentation.

audible – you can hear the sound.

inaudible – you can't hear the sound.

audition – the ability to hear; also a performance carried out for the purpose of evaluating an entertainer.

audit – an official examination and verification of records or conditions.

auditor – the person who does an audit; also a person who attends a class just to listen and not to work or get credit.

audio frequency – the range of human hearing, from 15 hertz (Hz), as in the lowest drumbeat, to 20,000 Hz, as in the highest squeak or note of birdsong.

Activities

Who tests your hearing?

Where do you go to hear speeches?

If you can't hear a sound, it is _____.

What is the range of human hearing?

Syllabification for correct spelling
_____
au-di-om-e-try

52 collate /koh late /kə lāt'

To *collate* means to place in order. It is often used to mean putting a group of papers in the proper order.

The prefix *col-* means "with" or "jointly" and the root *loca* means "place." So, to *collate* sort of means "with placement."

Col- is a version of the common prefix *co-*, which means "with." *Co-* has a habit of picking up the beginning consonant letter of some roots, such as those beginning with *n, m, r,* or *l,* and doubling the first letter of the root, as in *committee, correct, connect,* or *collocate.* (See Appendix C, on prefixes.)

Root
loca means "place."

local – nearby, as in "Go to a *local* store"; also a person who lives or was born nearby.

allocate – to place aside or request a distribution: "Congress has *allocated* money for education." (*al-* = to)

allocation or **allotment** – the money or a share of something set aside or distributed.

locus – a place or center of activities: "The *locus* of trouble is here." In geometry it can be a point where several lines cross. *Loci* is the plural of *locus.*

dislocate – to put anything out of place; used particularly to refer to body joints that are out of place or not working properly.

Activities

Will your photocopier *collate* multiple copies?

Have you ever received an *allotment*?

Name some joints that can *dislocate*.

What is the plural of *locus*?

Syllabification for correct spelling

_____

col-late

53 occlude /uh klewd /ə klo͞od'

To *occlude* means to "shut" or "stop up." You don't want to have an *occluded* artery, which shuts off blood flow and can cause a stroke or heart attack. Dentists determine whether your teeth *occlude,* or whether you have an *occlusion,* meaning whether your jaw shuts properly and your teeth line up. Weather forecasters look for *occluded* fronts, in which cold air shuts out warm and moves it up and away from the ground.

Root
clude means "shut."

conclude – to shut off a debate or end a performance or other action. (*con-* = with)

seclude – to shut off the outside world in order to achieve peace and privacy. (*se-* = shall)

exclude – to shut out or keep out. (*ex-* = from)

include – the opposite of *exclude.* (*in-* = in)

recluse – somebody who shuts off himself or herself, such as a monk or a person who just likes to be alone. (*re-* = back)

Activities

If an *occluded* front comes your way tomorrow, will the temperature become warmer or colder?

What do you call the last song at a concert?

A person who never comes out of her house is a
_____.

If your teeth do not come together normally, they do not _____.

Syllabification for correct spelling

_____

oc-clude

Ductile means "capable of being formed or pliable" and may refer to a material or to a person: "The soft clay was *ductile* in the hands of the sculptor." "Heated glass is *ductile* and can be pulled into fine threads." "Dictators hope for a *ductile* population."

aqueduct – an open, man-made passageway for channeling flowing water: "Drinking water comes from Northern California to Southern California in an *aqueduct*." (*aqua-* = water)

Root
duct means "lead."

viaduct – a bridge or elevated road built on piers or towers consisting of short spans: "The *viaduct* carried the road over the swampland." (*via-* = road)

conduct – to carry out a task: "She *conducts* her business in the office." "A class with bad *conduct* gets a grouchy teacher." (*con-* = with)

deduct – to take away from the total; to subtract: "Taxes are *deducted* from your pay." (*de-* = from)

abduct – to take or lead a person away by force: "Terrorists *abduct* both adults and children." (*ab-* = from)

Activities

Ancient Rome had *aqueducts* so that the population could have

_____.

Is modeling clay *ductile*?

Bad spelling might _____ from your essay grade.

Kidnappers _____ rich people.

What is another word for *bridge*?

Syllabification for correct spelling

_____

duc-tile

Ducal means "belonging to the *duke*," so it refers to the duke's house (manor) and farmlands. A duke is a leader and a part of the monarch system of government who ranks below a king or prince but above a baron or knight. Historically, a duke rules or leads a *duchy,* which is usually a large section of the kingdom that includes many villages. His wife is called a *duchess* and may help to run the *ducal* estate.

Root

duc is a form of *duct,* meaning "lead."

reduce – to shrink or diminish in size or number. (*re-* = back)

deduce – to draw a conclusion; to infer. (*de-* = from)

seduce – to persuade or lead astray, perhaps into disobedience, sometimes of a sexual nature. (*se-* = without)

produce – to bring or lead forth; a person can *produce* a play or a manuscript, a family can *produce* children. May also mean vegetables or what a farmer has *produced.* (*pro-* = forward)

induce – to lead by persuasion or influence. A salesperson can *induce* a customer to buy; a teacher can *induce* a student to learn. *Induce* also applies to the effects of substances; for example, drugs can *induce* sleepiness, or an electrical current can *induce* magnetism. (*in-* = in)

Activities

Who owns a *ducal* farm?

After hearing the facts, you can _____ an answer.

Someone trying to lose weight is trying to

_____.

The person who finances and works to bring out a new play is called a _____.

Syllabification for correct spelling

_____

du-cal

56 equanimity /ee kwuh nim i tee /ē' kwə nim' i tē

Equanimity means keeping an emotional balance even while under stress: "She accepted failure with *equanimity*." "Jose was hotheaded, but Maria responded with *equanimity*."

Animus could also be translated as "having life"—an animal is alive.

equator – the virtual line around the Earth that divides it into two equal-sized parts: the Northern Hemisphere and the Southern Hemisphere.

Root
equa means "equal"; *anim*, from the Latin *animus,* means "mind" or "soul."

equation – in algebra, a mathematical statement that has two equal mathematical expressions separated by an *equals sign* (=). *Equation* can also be used outside of mathematics: "Diplomats worry about the *equation* of power."

equality – sameness in quality, number, power, or status: "Racial *equality* means everybody gets treated *equally*."

equinox – when the sun crosses the equator or at noon appears directly overhead to somebody standing on the equator. At these times, the day and night are of equal length all over the Earth. The *vernal equinox* is when the sun moving north crosses the equator, about March 21; this is the first day of spring. When the sun moving south crosses the equator, about September 23, it is called the *autumnal equinox* and is the first day of fall. (*nox-* = night)

Activities

Somebody who "keeps his cool" has _____.

What separates the Northern and Southern Hemispheres?

What determines the change of seasons?

Is there racial *equality* in your community?

Syllabification for correct spelling

_____
e-qua-nim-i-ty

57 salient /say lee ent / sā' lē ənt

Salient means "prominent" or "outstanding," describing something that leaps out at you: "His *salient* feature was his big nose." "The *salient* point of his argument was false." *Salient* can also mean, literally, "leap." "A deer is a *salient* animal." "Frogs are *salient* amphibians." "A *salient* spring leaps out of winter in a sudden burst of sunshine."

Root
sal or *sult* means "to take."

salacious – bad, rude, indecent, offensive, or lewd; off-color and not polite: "In school, don't use *salacious* remarks, such as 'Her butt is too big!'"

salmon – a fish that leaps out of the water when swimming upstream to reproduce.

insult – to leap upon someone verbally rather than with fists or guns; a put-down; an attempt to offend a person or to make him or her feel angry or ashamed: "You're too stupid to understand."

result – a leap to the end, the outcome, the final action, the thing brought about by preceding activity.

Activities

What is a *salient* feature of your town?

Identify a *salient* amphibian.

What could you call a disrespectful remark?

The end of a process of reasoning is the

_____.

Syllabification for correct spelling

_____

sa-li-ent

58 lithosphere /lith oh sfeer /lith' ə sfēr'

The *lithosphere* is the hard-rock portion of the Earth's crust, descending to about sixty miles beneath the planet's surface. Below the *lithosphere* is the hot liquid rock of the Earth's center. Sometimes this hot liquid rock oozes out and erupts through cracks in the *lithosphere*, creating what we call a volcano; the liquid rock is then called lava. What we stand on, and what mountains are made of, is the *lithosphere*. *Litho* means "rock."

A ball is *spheroid* shaped. Sometimes poets or even ordinary writers refer to the Earth as "the sphere." Here are some other *sphere* words:

Root
sphere
means "round shape."

atmosphere – the layer of gasses surrounding the Earth, which go up about 135 miles. (*atmo-* = vapor) The *atmosphere* is also classified in various layers.

troposphere – the lowest layer of the atmosphere surrounding the Earth. It goes from 0 to about 7 miles up. We usually call this layer *air* and it is about 20 percent oxygen gas and about 80 percent nitrogen gas. The *troposphere* gets colder as it goes up and contains nearly all of the clouds and weather. (*trop-* = turn or change)

stratosphere – the next layer of the Earth's atmosphere. It goes from 7 to 25 miles up. It contains no weather and its temperature does not change much. (*strat-* = spread out)

Activities

What layer of the Earth do you drive your car on?

What layer of the *atmosphere* do you breathe?

Is the upper *stratosphere* colder than the lower *stratosphere*?

When liquid rock flows out of a crack in the *lithosphere*, we call it _____.

Syllabification for correct spelling
_____
lith-o-sphere

59 encryption /en kript shun /en krip' shən

Encryption means using secret codes to rearrange the written message so that only a person who knows the key to the codes can read it. The idea of using codes has been around a long time. Julius Caesar used a simple one of substituting each letter with a letter three places down in the alphabet, so "Julius" becomes "MXOLXV." In World War II the Germans used a very complicated code called Enigma that had sextillion combinations. A sextillion is 1,000,000,000,000,000, 000,000. The allies cracked the code using a computer.

Root

crypt means "hidden"; the prefix *en-* means "in."

cryptogram – a message written in a secret code by a *cryptographer*.

cryptanalysis – the solving of unknown codes or the development of new ones.

cryptocrystalline – a geology term meaning that the structure of a rock has crystals so fine that they cannot be seen using an ordinary microscope. This is an example of a scientific word using the *crypt* root.

Besides being a root, *crypt* is also a word.

crypt – a vault or underground chamber, often a burial place under the floor of a church, sometimes used for saints or important persons.

encrypt – to put in a *crypt*: "The body was *encrypted*." (*en-* = in)

Activities

Try writing a short *cryptogram* using Caesar's code.

If you do this, will you be a *cryptographer*?

Where were some old saints buried?

What are tiny rock crystals called?

Syllabification for correct spelling

en-cryp-tion

60 just /just /just

Vocabulary learning is not all learning new words. It is also learning more meanings for words you already know. Let's take a look at a simple four-letter word: *just*.

1. **just** – by a small amount: "He got to class *just* in time."

2. **just** – exactly: "The temperature is *just* right."

3. **just** – reasonable: "The counteroffer *was* just."

4. **just** – merited: "She received a *just* reward for her hard work."

Root
just often has to do with correctness, rightness, or law.

just-in-time – part of a manufacturing process in which materials are not kept in inventory but delivered exactly when needed.

justice – fairness: "*Justice* was done by the long sentence."

Justice – a type of judge: a U.S. Supreme Court *Justice* or a *Justice* of the Peace of a small town.

justify – vindicate: "His actions were *justified* in the end."

justify – to line up or square: "The right-hand margin of the type in most books and newspapers is *justified*. Conversely, the right-hand margin in most letters and unpublished written papers is *unjustified* or ragged." This page has an *unjustified* right margin.

Activities

Give an example of an *unjust* reward.

What's another name for a judge?

Look at any book and see if the margins are *justified*.

Have you had to *justify* something that you did?

Syllabification for correct spelling

_____

just

61 dichotomy /die kot uh mee /dī kot' ə mē

A *dichotomy* is a division of something into two parts, sometimes into two opposing groups: "There is a basic *dichotomy* between things good and things evil."

It is similar to the common prefix di-, which also means "two." The root *tomy* appears in a number of words, such as:

Root

tomy or *tom* means "cut." The prefix *dich-* means "in two."

atom – In general, an *atom* is a tiny or very small part. So you could talk about "a glass smashed into *atoms*." But in physics or chemistry an *atom* has a very exact definition: the smallest particle of an element that can exist alone. (*a-* = to)

anatomy – the structure of a plant or an animal, as well as the art of studying this structure. "Human *anatomy* is the naming and detailed description of human body parts." (*ana-* = up)

Doctors use *tomy* in words to name all sorts of operations that cut out all or part of various organs:

tonsillectomy = removal of tonsils   **appendectomy** = removal of appendix

mastoidectomy = removal of mastoid   **gastrectomy** = removal of part or all of stomach

Activities

Change *dichotomy* into a verb. (Note: use the ending "*ize.*")

Now use the verb in a sentence.

Do a poet and a chemist mean the same thing when they use the word *atom*?

If you have your appendix cut out, what is the operation called?

Syllabification for correct spelling
_____
di-chot-o-my

Someone who is *despondent* is depressed, dejected, discouraged, forlorn, hopeless, desperate, or otherwise not very happy: "I lost my job and I have no hope of getting another one. Besides that, neither my dog nor my girlfriend will speak to me. That is why I am *despondent*."

Root
spond or *spons* means "to pledge."

sponsor – one who pledges support or backup for another person or event. For example, congressmen *sponsor* a new law, and old club members may *sponsor* a new member.

respond – to answer, reply, or act after some stimulus: "He wrote to her but she didn't *respond*." "She was so mad that she wouldn't *respond* to the phone call." (*re-* = back)

responsible – trustworthy, *responsive* when called, accepting of trust: "Who is *responsible* for this mess?"

correspondent – one who writes letters or news stories from distant places: "She was the newspaper's *correspondent* in China." "My pen pal is my best correspondent." (*cor-* = with) (See Appendix C, on prefixes.)

irresponsible – not being responsible: "He's so *irresponsible* that he never shows up on time or finishes the job he is supposed to do." (*ir-* = not; used only if root begins with *r*; otherwise, *un-* is used.)

Activities

Have you ever been *despondent*?

Has anyone ever *sponsored* you?

A TV newscaster sent to Asia is a

_____.

Would you hire someone who is *irresponsible*?

Syllabification for correct spelling
_____
de-spond-ent

Portage commonly refers to the awkward business of carrying a boat when the boat should be carrying you. For example, if you are peacefully paddling your canoe down a stream and you come to a waterfall, you'd better take the canoe out of the water and *portage* it around the falls. *Portage* can also mean carrying a load on a trail. *Porters* carry luggage and other items.

Root
port means "to carry."

import – to bring things into a country or other area. (*im-* = in)

export – to carry things out of a country or other area. (*ex-* = out)

transport – to carry things from one place to another. (*trans-* = across)

support – to uphold, help to maintain, assist: "A pole helped to support the sagging ceiling." "He *supported* his mother by getting a job." (*sup-* is a version of *sub-*; both mean "under.") (See Appendix C.)

report – to carry back information (*re-* = back)

portfolio – a group of papers or a flat case for carrying them. An artist looking for a job shows her *portfolio,* a sample of her best work. An investor has a *portfolio* of stocks. (*folio-* = leaf)

port – This simple word has a number of meanings. It can mean a harbor where ships carry in goods. It can mean the left side of a ship—historically the side usually tied to the dock. It can also mean an entry or door to a building. *Port* is also a type of wine originally from Portugal, or it can be a connection place on a computer.

Activities

Carrying a boat over land is called a _____.

Goods leaving a country are called _____.

Would you like to have a *portfolio* of stocks?

Which side of a ship is the *port* side?

Syllabification for correct spelling

_____

por-tage

Cyclonic means related to or having the characteristics of a cycle or wheel. It is used most frequently in the phrase *cyclonic storm.* In a *cyclonic* storm the winds blow around a center with a diameter of perhaps hundreds of miles. *Cyclonic* storms in which the wind speed can exceed a hundred miles per hour are called by different names in different places:

Root
cycle means "wheel" or "reoccurring event," as in *business cycle.*

hurricane – a *cyclonic* storm starting in the southern Atlantic Ocean that sometimes hits the United States on the Atlantic or Gulf Coast.

typhoon – a *cyclonic* storm in the western Pacific region, such as in Japan, China, or the Philippines.

cyclone – a *cyclonic* storm on land in the United States or in the Indian Ocean.

willy willies – *cyclonic* storms that occur off the northern coast of Australia.

The root *cycle* is used in the names of common vehicles, such as:

unicycle – one-wheeled vehicle (*uni-* = one)

bicycle – two-wheeled vehicle (*bi-* = two)

tricycle – three-wheeled vehicle (*tri-* = three)

motorcycle – motor-driven bicycle

Activities

Where you live, what is a *cyclonic* storm called?

If you lived in Japan, what would you call a *cyclonic* storm?

What other things are *cyclonic* or have *cycles*?

Name some *hurricanes* (they always have human first names, all female one year and all male the next).

Syllabification for correct spelling
_____
cy-clon-ic

65 pathos /pay thoss /pā' thos

Pathos is a feeling of pity or sympathetic sorrow. It is often a characteristic of a play, as in "The last act was loaded with *pathos*."

pathetic – sad or even hopeless; can apply to a person or situation.

sympathy – an inclination to feel or think like another. Whatever affects one person affects the other: "I gave my friend *sympathy* when her sister died." (*sym-* = with)

pathology – the study of illness or diseases. (*-ology* = study of)

Root
path means "suffer."

allopathy – a system of medicine that attempts to use all measures that have proven effective. Most modern medical doctors (MDs) consider themselves *allopaths*. *Allopathic* medicine aims to combat disease by using remedies different from the disease. Aspirin is an allopathic medicine. (*all-* = all)

homeopathy – a system of medicine, used more in the past, that treats disease by giving as a remedy a minute bit of a substance that, if administered in quantity to a healthy person, would produce symptoms of the disease. If you had a fever, a *homeopathic* physician would give you a tiny bit of medicine that would normally raise your temperature. (*homo-* = same)

Activities

When you visit a friend in the hospital, you often give them some _____.

How would you describe a cold, wet dog that is lost?

Most of the medicines in a drug store are used in the _____ system of medicine.

Have you seen a play or TV series that made you feel *pathos*?

Syllabification for correct spelling
_____
pa-thos

Invincible means cannot be beaten, subdued, or conquered. An *invincible* army or football team just can't lose. An *invincible* fortress is secure. An *invincible* argument will win the debate.

The prefix *in-* means "not," so *invincible* literally means "cannot be conquered." (Unfortunately *in-* sometimes also means "in," as in *insight*.)

Root
vinc (also spelled *vint*) means "conquer."

victor – one who conquers or wins a contest. *Victor* is also a boy's name, and *Victoria* is a girl's name. Both are winners. The suffix *-or* and the suffix *-ia* both mean "a person" or "one who."

convince – to persuade by evidence or argument; historically, "to conquer." (*con-* = with)

province – part of a country; historically, the part of the empire that was conquered or taken in war.

convict – a prisoner, someone *convicted* of a crime. (*con-* = with)

evict – to put someone out of a property by legal process; historically, *eviction* by force may have been more common. (*e-* = out)

Activities

Name a team that you hope is *invincible*.

Tell a person named *Victor* or *Victoria* what his or her name means.

What is the difference between the old and new meanings of *convince*?

What is a *province*?

Syllabification for correct spelling

_____

in-vin-ci-ble

Philanthropy is an act of generosity—frequently, giving money to a good cause that will help other people. There are many instances of large-scale *philanthropy,* such as Andrew Carnegie's funding of the start up of libraries around the United States, or Bill and Melinda Gates's setting up of a foundation that addresses AIDS, education, and other worthwhile causes.

Root
phil means "love."

philosophy – the love or pursuit of wisdom. (*soph-* = wisdom or knowledge)

philharmonic – a musical organization or the orchestra it sponsors, for example, the New York *Philharmonic* Orchestra. (*harmonic* = harmony)

Philadelphia – city name meaning "brotherly love."

philander – to make love in a trifling or fickle way (not seriously), perhaps with many different women; historically it meant to love men (what today we might call homosexual behavior). (*ander-* = men)

bibliophile – a lover of books. (*biblio-* = book)

anglophile – a lover of England or English ways. *anglo-* comes from *Angloterra,* the old name for England, which came from the old European tribe the Anglo-Saxons. (*terra-* = land)

Frankophile – lover of the French or French ways. The Franks were an old European tribe that inhabited what we now call France.

Activities

Who are some local *philanthropists*?

Someone who regularly goes to the library
   may be a _____.

Someone who loves England is
   an _____.

What is the name of a major symphonic
   orchestra in a large city near you?

Syllabification for correct spelling
_____
phi-lan-thro-py

A *unicorn* is a mythical animal with one horn in the middle of its forehead whose body is a mixture of horse and stag (male deer). It is mentioned in the ancient literature of Greece, India, and China. Most real animals, such as cows and deer, have two horns and thus are *bicorned*. (*corn-* = horn)

universe – an entire body of things. It commonly means all the stars, planets, and galaxies, but it can apply to other collections as well. (*verse-* = turn)

Prefix
uni means "one."

university – a body of scholars who come together to instruct students and do research: "In the United States, a *university* is the highest level of the educational system."

universal – covering everything within a universe. *Universal* education means everybody gets educated.

unique – one of a kind: "That dress is *unique*."

union – joining two or more things together to form one: "*Unions* join together all of the workers so they can bargain for better conditions."

uniform – of the same form as others; identical clothing worn by members of a particular group: "Companies follow *uniform* procedures so that all branches carry out the same tasks in the same way." "Members of the army wear *uniforms;* all of the soldiers dress the same."

unit – a group of persons or things that are counted as one; a person or thing that is part of a larger whole: "A *unit* of state government is the county; some states consist of ten or more counties." "A car is composed of hundreds of *units*."

Activities

Name some *bicorned* animals.

What are some *units* of a university?

Name some *unique* things.

Besides clothes, what other things can be *uniform*?

Syllabification for correct spelling

u-ni-corn

A *eulogy* is a speech or written essay praising a person or act. It is frequently part of a funeral service, when the minister and friends say some good words about the deceased.

apology – an expression of regret for a fault committed. (*apo-* = away or off)

analogy – a likeness or sameness between things that are otherwise different: "An *analogy* for life is a rose, which buds, blooms, makes fruit and seeds, then dies." (*ana-* = again)

Root
log comes from Greek and can mean simply "word" or "speech."

epilogue – the concluding section or speech of a novel or play: "The *epilogue* given by an actor made sense of the whole play."

log – a book of daily entries of a ship's position, or any type of journal: "She kept a *log* of her activities."

log on – to sign on to a system using identifying information: "She used her screen name and a password to *log on* to the Internet."

The Greeks equated words and speech with reasoning, so the root *logy* also meant "knowledge" or "science of." (A variation, *logos*, was sometimes used to mean God.)

logic – the science of correct reasoning: "That view of things seems *logical* to me."

psychology – the science of or reasoning about the mind or mental phenomena. The *-ology* ending is also used in such words as *biology,* the science of living organisms (*bio-* = life), and *lexicology* the science of the meaning and use of words. (*lex-* = words) (See Appendix D.)

Activities

Have you ever heard a *eulogy*?

Make up an *analogy*.

Who judges what is *logical*?

List a bunch of words ending in *-ology*.

Syllabification for correct spelling

———————

eu-lo-gy

Intractable means "not easily moved, taught, or trained." *Intractable* persons are obstinate; you can't change their minds. They don't want to learn anything new. They don't want to change their behavior. *Intractable* can also apply to other things. For example, an illness can be *intractable* and not respond to any medicine, or a metal can be *intractable* and not easily be bent or formed.

Root
tract means to "pull" or "drag."

tractor – a vehicle that pulls something. On a farm a *tractor* may pull a plow, and on the highway the *tractor* part of a truck pulls the trailer part. (-*or* = one who)

attract – to pull toward: "An *attractive* girl pulls a lot of boys toward her." (*at-* is a form of the prefix *a-*, which means "to") (See Appendix C, on prefixes.)

detract – to take away a part of something and thus diminish its importance or worth. For example, a flaw can *detract* from the value of an antique, or a spelling error can *detract* from the grade of a paper. (*de-* = from)

retract – take something back: "If I'm wrong, I'll *retract* that last statement." (*re-* = back)

traction – the act of pulling; adhesive friction: "New tires will give your car better *traction* on a wet road." "His broken leg was in *traction* and was being pulled so it would heal better."

Activities

Do you know somebody who is *intractable*?

What does a *tractor* do?

Have you ever *retracted* something?

Why does your car need *traction*?

Syllabification for correct spelling
_____
in-trac-ta-ble

Emit means "send out." Fire *emits* heat, the sun *emits* light, even people *emit* goodwill sometimes.

omit – to leave out something: "Do not *omit* the check when paying the bill, and do not *omit* a page of an important document." The prefix *o-* is a form of *ob-* and can mean "to" or "against."

admit – to permit entry: "You are *admitted* to school"; or to accept what is true: "The crook *admitted* to his crime." (*ad-* = to)

Root

mit means "send" and the prefix *e-* means "out."

remit – to release, cancel, or forgive: "The penalty was *remitted* and he didn't have to pay the fine." (*re-* = back)

permit – to consent or allow: "Smoking is not *permitted* in this building"; a document granting permission: "A *permit* from the city was required to add a new section to the building." (*per-* = through)

transmit – to cause something to be sent to another place or another person: "This radio station *transmits* only music." (*trans-* = across)

intermittent – not continuous; experiencing interruptions in the sending of something: "The radio signal was *intermittent* because of static." (*inter-* = between)

commit – to send someone to prison; to put in a permanent form: "You should *commit* that idea to writing." (*com-* = with)

submit – to yield to an authority: "You must *submit* to the laws or go to jail"; to present for consideration or review: "You can *submit* your article to the editor for possible publication." (*sub-* = under)

Activities

What does a radio tower *emit*?

What do dieters try to *omit*?

Is your attention in class *intermittent*?

Are you *committed* to something or somebody?

Syllabification for correct spelling

―――――――――

e-mit

Hydrogen is a basic element. It makes up 75 percent of the Universe. An element, or atom, is the smallest particle of matter, although modern atomic science is looking into smaller parts within the atom. *Hydrogen* is the simplest element because it has only one proton and one electron.

In Greek mythology, Hydra, the many-headed water serpent, had the unfortunate quality that when one of its heads was cut off, two more grew in its place. Hence the term *Hydra-headed monster* means that whenever you solve one problem, two more grow in its place.

Hydrogen is so-called because when hydrogen gas is burned it produces water.

Prefix
hydro- means "water."

hydrocarbon – any material based on the combination of a hydrogen and a carbon atom, such as gasoline, natural gas, and many other products that come from oil and coal. Environmentalists dislike hydrocarbon fuels because they are bad for the atmosphere and cause a few international problems.

hydrant – a pipe and valve used to get water from the main water supply, often called *fire hydrant*. (*-ant* = thing or person)

hydrology – the science of water, its distribution and properties in soil, on soil, in the atmosphere; evaporation, etc.

Activities

What atomic element has only one electron?

What is the root *hydro* named after?

Are there any *Hydra*-headed monsters in the news or in your life?

Why should we use fewer *hydrocarbon* fuels?

Syllabification for correct spelling

***

hy-dro-gen

73 moderator /mah der ray tor /mod' ə rā' tər

A *moderator* is a person who presides over a debate or discussion for the purpose of keeping the discussion within bounds or following the rules. In a dispute, the *moderator* can also be a *mediator,* which means someone between the two parties who seeks a middle ground. A judge might sometimes act as a *mediator,* but a judge's official job is to interpret and apply the law. Outside of the courtroom, a judge may act as a *moderator.* Teachers are often *moderators.*

Root
mod means "within bounds" or "manner."

modest – having a limited or not exaggerated opinion of one's worth; shy, not flashy: "She was dressed very modestly so as not to attract attention."

immodest – not modest; vulgar, in bad taste (*im-* = not)

modicum – a small or limited amount: "He paid a modicum of attention to his date."

mode – a common way of doing something. In fashion, the *mode* is "what everybody is wearing." In statistics, the *mode* is one kind of average. In a batch of raw scores on a test, the *mode* is the most common or frequent score, the score that occurs most often. It differs from the median score, which is the score in the middle of the ranked scores. It also differs from the mean or arithmetic average, which is all the scores added together then divided by the number of individual scores. *Mean, mode,* and *median* are sometimes called *average.*

modus operandi – a Latin phrase meaning "manner of operating." Modus operandi is the famous *MO* of detective stories, in which the detectives try to catch the crook by learning his usual manner of operating.

Activities

What is the difference between a *moderator* and a judge?

Describe a *modest* dress.

What is the difference between a *mode* and a *mean*?

What does *MO* mean?

Syllabification for correct spelling

---

mod-er-a-tor

A *barometer* is an instrument for measuring the pressure of the atmosphere. It is widely used in weather prediction. It can also be used to measure elevation above sea level, in which case it is called an *altimeter;* it is found in most airplanes. *Barometers* work as altimeters because atmospheric (air) pressure drops as elevation rises. *Barometers* aid in weather forecasting because changes in atmospheric pressure may mean that a storm is coming.

Root
meter means "measure"; *bar* means "weight" or "pressure."

metric system – a system of measurement developed in France and now used in many countries. Its basic unit of length is the **meter** (also spelled *metre*) which is one ten-millionth of the distance between the equator and the North Pole, or about 39.3 inches. By adding Latin prefixes, the *metric system* provides larger and smaller units of length:

Larger	Smaller
dekameter = 10 meters	**decimeter** = 1/10th meter
hectometer = 100 meters	**centimeter** = 1/100th meter
kilometer = 1000 meters	**millimeter** = 1/1000th meter

Other *meter* words include the following:

geometry – the mathematics of lines, points, and space (*geo-* = earth)

perimeter – the boundary or distance around a space (*peri-* = around)

Activities

How does an *altimeter* help a pilot?

Why did the French use the distance from the equator to the North Pole as a basis for developing a standard measure of length?

Is a *centimeter* larger than a *dekameter*?

What is the distance around a building called?

Syllabification for correct spelling
___
ba-rom-e-ter

A *republic* is a form of government that is headed not by a *monarch* (king or queen) but, usually, by a president. The main power resides in the citizens (in the United States, the Congress shares power with the president and the courts).

puberty – condition of being capable of producing a child; the biological time of sexual maturity.

Root
pub means "grown up" or "adult."

public – literally, adults; generally, all persons.

public school – in the United States, a school supported mainly by local and state taxes and open to or required for children in kindergarten through grade 12; in the United Kingdom, a *public school* is a privately owned school that charges tuition and has selective admittance policies. Historically, a UK public school was a step forward from individual tutors; it taught groups of children, hence it was more public. In the UK, a government-supported school open to all is often called a "council school."

publicity – making someone or something known to the public. If it is for commercial purposes it is often called *advertising*.

publication – issuing copies of a book, music score, etc., for the public. A book, magazine or newspaper.

public defender – a lawyer hired by the government to defend someone charged of a crime who does not have his or her own lawyer.

Activities

Identify some nations that have the word *republic* in their official name. (Check a map or almanac for the names of nations.)

What is the difference between a U.S. and a U.K. *public* school?

If you are broke and must go before a criminal court, what is your lawyer called?

Are there any *publications* near you right now?

Syllabification for correct spelling

---

re-pub-lic

76 hosteler /hahs tull er /hos' tl ər

A *hosteler* is an innkeeper, who takes care of a hotel and its guests. It is sometimes spelled and pronounced without the *h, osteler*. A *hosteler* can also refer to someone who stays in a hostel.

host – someone who entertains in his house or presides over a social gathering.

hostess – a female host; as with other feminizations, not always used anymore. (-*ess* = female suffix)

Root
host or *hosp*
means "host."

hostel – an inn or lodging place for travelers, particularly those who are young and don't have a large travel budget.

hotel – a building of rooms rented to travelers; a modern derivation of the word *hostel*.

hospitable – welcoming of guests and strangers; having a warm and friendly attitude.

hos- pital – a medical institution where sick people go for medical attention and generally stay overnight.

hostage – a person kept against his or her will, perhaps to force an exchange of prisoners or the extraction of money (as in a kidnapping). (A rather strange use of the root *host*.)

Activities

What is another word for an innkeeper?

Why is the suffix -*ess* being used less?

How are *hotel* and *hospital* related in meaning?

Who is the *host* for a *hostage*?

Syllabification for correct spelling

_____

hos-tel-er

A *hyperbole* is a statement of super or over exaggeration. A *hyperbole* is just too much, it's beyond reality: "The stranger was ten feet tall."

bolt – to flea suddenly. A horse may *bolt* and throw its rider to the ground; a candidate may *bolt* from his political party. An original meaning for *bolt* was a shaft shot from a crossbow, which certainly was thrown out suddenly. As a noun, a *bolt* can be a bar of metal to hold a door closed, or a threaded shaft used to attach something to metal with a threaded nut. A *bolt* can also be a length of cloth or wallpaper rolled in a bundle.

Root
hyper means "over" or "excessive"; *bol* means "throw."

parabola – a special kind of U-shaped curve with a focal point that reflects parallel lines. For example, in a headlight, the bulb is the focal point and the reflector is a *parabolic curve,* so the rays are sent out parallel and maximum light is shone on a confined area. Many telescopes use a *parabolic mirror* to focus incoming light rays onto a viewing point. (*para-* = beside)

parable – a short story with a moral or a religious theme used for teaching a principle. (*para* = beside, alongside)

diabolical – pertaining to the devil. (*dia-* = through or across)

symbol – something that represents something else: "An alphabet letter is a *symbol* for a speech sound." (*sym-* or *syn-* = with or together)

Activities

Make up your own *hyperbole* for something.

What are three meanings for *bolt*?

Does a flashlight use a *parabolic* curve?

Are Aesop's Fables *parables*?

Syllabification for correct spelling
_____
hy-per-bo-le

Something that is *evident* is easily seen; it's obvious, it's easily understood: "It was *evident* from the ring on her finger that she was married."

evidence – something that can be shown or said in a trial as proof of guilt or innocence. The prefix *e-* can mean "out," so *evidence* is something that is out where it can be seen.

Root
vid or *vis* means "see."

visit – to spend time with a friend; a social call; a short-term residence; to go to a place for business or pleasure.

visitor – someone who visits. (suffix *-or* = person who)

vista – a distant view: "The *vista* of the mountains was superb."

television – an electronic device that receives electronic signals and displays them visually and auditorially. The root *tele* means "far," so *television* means "seeing from afar."

revise – to look back at something (often your own writing) and change it, hopefully for the better. You then have a *revision*.

advise – to counsel or offer help with a problem or situation: "The *adviser* is someone who perhaps can see the situation a little more clearly." (*ad-* = to)

provide – to supply what is needed; to take precautionary action.

provisions – supplies, especially those needed for a journey. The prefix *pro-* means "for" or "before," so you *see ahead* when you gather *provisions*.

Activities

What is the role of *evidence* in a murder trial?

What is a good *vista* in your area?

What sorts of things can you do when you *revise* a story?

List some *provisions* for a picnic.

Syllabification for correct spelling
_____
ev-i-dent

Hypothermia is a below-normal body temperature. Just feeling cold is not *hypothermia,* but people lost in a snow storm or who stay out in the bitter cold for a long time can experience an abnormal cooling of the body. A little *hypothermia* will not permanently hurt a person. In fact, doctors do it to a patient before a heart operation. But too much *hypothermia* will kill a person. *Hypothermia* rather than drowning is probably what killed passengers of the *Titanic* who went overboard into the cold Atlantic Ocean.

Root
hypo means "under"; *therm* means "heat."

Hypo- is a common Greek combining form, especially in the field of medicine:

hypodermic – needle used to administer an injection of medicine under the skin. (*derm-* = skin)

hypotension – low blood pressure. (*ten* = stretch)

hypotrophy – lack of growth or degeneration of a part of the body due to loss of cells. (*-trophy* = growth)

thermometer – an instrument used to measure heat. (*meter* = measure)

thermostat – a device used to regulate heat. You probably have one in your living room. The root *stat* means "stand," so a thermostat causes the heat in a room to "stand" at a set level.

thermodynamics – a branch of physics that deals with the relationship between heat, work, and energy. (*dynam* = power)

Activities

What kills people trapped in cold water?

Have you had a *hypodermic* injection?

What will a *thermometer* tell you?

How will you probably feel if you have *hypotension*?

Syllabification for correct spelling

hy-po-ther-mi-a

Something that is *innate* is present at birth—is inborn, hereditary, or congenital. To have an *innate* ability means that you did not have to work or study to get it; you were just born that way. Some people, for example, have *innate* musical ability. However, *innate* abilities can be improved with education and practice.

Root
nat means "born."

native – someone or something born in a certain region. A *native* person is one born in a particular city or village. A *native* plant is one that has always grown in a particular region. In contrast, an *exotic* plant was introduced into the region from the outside.

prenatal – something occurring before birth: "Drinking alcohol while pregnant can cause *prenatal* problems with the child, resulting in serious lifelong problems such as cerebral palsy."

nature – the unchanged, original state of the world: "He gets out into the forest to be with *nature*"; basic characteristics of a creature or thing: "It is his *nature* to be friendly." (suffix *-ure* = action or process)

naturalize – to confer the citizenship rights of a native person onto an alien; to adapt or grow like a native: "Plants from a distant area can become *naturalized*." (The suffix *-ize* makes a word a verb.)

nation – a section of the Earth that has its own government. Originally a *nation* was a group of people of similar birth or race. (The suffix *-tion* makes a word a noun.)

supernatural – beyond the physical or observable universe; applied to God, spirits, religious beliefs. (*super-* = over, beyond)

Activities

Do you know someone with an *innate* ability?

Can you point out a *native* plant and an exotic plant?

What influences a child *prenatally*?

What is the *United Nations*?

Syllabification for correct spelling

—————————
in-nate

81 regent /ree jent /rē' jənt

A *regent* is a ruler, such as a king or someone acting for the king, a university official, or a member of a governing board. In any event, it is someone invested with authority who makes sure that the rules are kept.

regime /reh zheem/ – a form of government or method of ruling. For example, the Nazi *regime* was a government ruled by the dictator Adolf Hitler.

Root
gen means "rule."

regimen /rej uh men/ – a regular or rule-governed pattern of occurrence or action: "My doctor prescribed a *regimen* of one dose of medication daily." "The weather pattern in my region includes a *regimen* of storms each fall."

region – a particular part of the Earth or universe, often characterized by a distinctive feature, for example, a tropical or arctic *region*, or the *region* of stars known as Sirius. Originally a *region* was an area ruled by a Roman governor.

regular – governed by rules, orderly, methodical, normal, standard, customary. (*-ular* – related to)

irregular – not regular. (prefix *ir-* = not) (See Appendix C, on prefixes.)

regiment – a large body of soldiers ruled by a colonel, consisting of various units such as companies, batteries, and battalions.

Activities

What does a *regent* do?

What is a *regime*?

Name some different kinds of *regions*.

Is a battalion larger than a *regiment*?

Syllabification for correct spelling

_____

re-gent

Real is a word we use so often that we seldom think about it. *Real* is commonly used as an adjective, which means it modifies a noun. It can mean "not artificial," as in *real gold.* It might also mean "something permanent or fixed," as in *real estate,* or it might mean "everyday life," as in the *real world.* It is used, too, for emphasis, as in "real danger."

When *re-* is used as a *prefix,* however, it means "back," as in *return* or *reapply.*

Root
real means "thing."

realize – to cause or perceive something to be *real*: "The loan he obtained helped him to *realize* his dreams." "Because of what you did, I now *realize* you care."

realization – The suffix *-ation* changes the verb *realize* into a noun: "The *realization* shocked me." This is a word with three suffixes: *-al* (adjective), *-ize* (verb), and *-ation* (noun). It shows the important part that suffixes play in grammar, particularly in changing parts of speech.

real estate – property in the form of land and buildings.

realty /ree uhl tee/ – a synonym for real estate. A real estate office could also be called a *realty* office.

reality /ree al it tee/ – the quality or state of being real. Notice the shift in pronunciation and meaning with the addition of one letter. The suffix *-ity* means "state or quality of," but more important, it changes the word into a noun. A lot of suffixes emphasize grammar over meaning.

Activities

What is gold that is not *real*?

What is the most common meaning of *re-*?

Change some nouns into verbs using *-ize*.

What is a synonym for *real estate*?

> **Syllabification for correct spelling**
> ———————
> **re-al**

The word *stance* can be used in two ways. First, it can mean a physical position or posture: "The golfer took a firm stance before swinging his club." Second, it can mean a mental or emotional attitude: "She took a firm *stance* against the war."

So, "What is your *stance*?" can mean, "How are you standing?" or "What is your position?"

Root
sta means "stand."

stand – to be in an upright posture or to take a fixed position (verb); a structure such as a booth for selling things or a raised platform for a band (noun).

obstacle – anything that hinders or obstructs: "The path had many *obstacles*, such as low branches." (*ob-* = against)

standard – something established as a basis for comparison; the usual or normal. Originally a *standard* was a pole with a flag on it. (*-ard* = noun)

stage – a platform for plays or performances. Originally it stood above the audience.

statue – a carved or molded form of a person, animal, or other object. It stands still.

stamina – resistance to fatigue; ability to stay or stand for a long period.

station – a place where something is located, such as a gas *station*; a stopping or waiting (standing) place, such as a train *station*.

Also check out *state, status, stay, substantial, staid*, and *understand*.

Activities

Describe something on which you have taken a *stance*.

What are some *standards* you know about?

What requires *stamina*?

Identify several uses of *standard*.

Syllabification for correct spelling

_____

stance

84 substitute /sub stih toot /sub' sti tōōt'

A *substitute* is a person or thing that stands in the place of another. A *substitute* teacher stands in for the regular teacher; when a football player is injured, a *substitute* takes his place; and if you can't find real butter, you can use *substitute* butter.

The reason that roots that come from the same Latin word are sometimes spelled a little different is that they are variant forms of the Latin word. Variant forms in English are *run* and *ran*, for example, which have similar meanings but are in different tenses.

Root
sub means "under"; *stit* means "stand" just as *sta* did in the previous lesson.

destitute – very poor, without even the necessities of life. (*de-* = from)

constitute – to set up, establish, or make up: "Strong winds *constituted* a major part of the storm." (*con-* = with)

constitution – the noun form of constitute: "He had a healthy *constitution*." Also, a body of laws or rules. When capitalized, it usually means the *Constitution* of the United States.

restitution – making good any loss or injury: "For *restitution*, the crook paid back all he had stolen." (*re-* = back)

solstice – when the sun stands still in its declination (apparent movement from north to south or south to north), Dec. 21 and June 21, the shortest and longest days of the year, respectively. (*sol-* = sun)

Activities

Describe several types of *substitutes*.

What are the variant forms of *go*?

What does capitalization do for *constitution*?

When is *restitution* called for?

> **Syllabification for correct spelling**
> _____
> **sub-sti-tute**

85 evolve /ee vahlv /i volv'

Evolve is a verb that means "to work out or develop something." An author can *evolve* a plan for a novel, a scientist can *evolve* a theory, and shaky governments can *evolve* into steady governments.
So *evolve* literally means to roll out something.

evolution – the noun form of *evolve:* "We talked about the *evolution* of his plan." By itself, *evolution* frequently refers to Darwin's theory in biology of how species have developed.

Root
vol means to "roll"; *e-* means "out."

revolt – a turning away from a leader or government: "A *revolt* was brewing among the soldiers"; to disgust or shock: "The sight of so much blood *revolted* me." (*re-* = back)

revolution – the violent overthrow of a government. *Revolution* can also be a journey around something: "The Earth makes one *revolution* around the sun every year" and "This machine part can make thirty *revolutions* per minute."

revolver – a gun with a *revolving* (turning) chamber that holds bullets.

volume – a book, often part of a larger work: "Encyclopedias have many *volumes*." In ancient times, a *volume* was a scroll that was part of a larger written work. *Volume* can also mean an amount of space: "What is the *volume* of that tank?" And it can mean loudness: "Turn that *volume* down!"

involve – to draw in as a participant: "Don't get *involved* in their fight"; to get entangled: "His brother has *involved* him in all of his business decisions." (*in-* = in)

Activities

Identify a *revolution* going on now.

Identify a series that has many *volumes*.

How can you get *involved* in politics?

What does the root *vol* mean?

Syllabification for correct spelling

---

e-volve

To *erupt* means to release or force out suddenly and perhaps even violently. Volcanos *erupt* through the surface of the Earth with a violent issue of lava and hot gas. A human being can *erupt* into a temper tantrum.

So an *eruption* is a "breakout."

rupture – break: "The Earth's surface was *ruptured* by the earthquake." "Our bodies get *ruptures* in the form of torn muscles and exploding appendixes."

Root
rupt means "break"; *e-* means "out."

corrupt – to change something from good to bad. Politicians and businessmen, for example, can become *corrupt* and steal money or do other illegal things. (The prefix *cor-* is a variation of *com-* and means "with.")

interrupt – to stop or break into a continuing action. For example, applause or cat calls can *interrupt* a speech, and lightning can *interrupt* electrical service. (*inter-* = between)

abrupt – to break off or cause a sudden ending. For example, hanging up can *abruptly* end a phone conversation, and a meeting or song can have an *abrupt* ending. (*ab-* = from)

disrupt – to break apart. For example, a gas line can be *disrupted* by an earthquake, a classroom can be *disrupted* by loud talking, and the road system can be *disrupted* by a storm. (*dis-* = apart)

Activities

Can you recall any volcano *eruptions*?

What is the latest *corruption* scandal in the newspapers?

Have any services to your house been *interrupted*?

What can doctors do about *ruptures*?

Syllabification for correct spelling
_____
e-rupt

Obverse means "opposite" and is frequently used in describing a coin or a paper monetary note: "When you flip a coin, heads is the obverse of tails." *Obverse* can also apply to opposite sides of a discussion, idea, debate, or opposing team: "The *obverse* of the positive side is the negative side."

So *obverse* can mean to "turn against" or "turn over." To add a little bit of confusion, the prefix *ob-* can also mean "to" or "toward."

Root
vers means "turn"; *ob-* means "against" or "over."

versatile – having the ability to turn easily or to do many different things: "He was so *versatile* that he could play both the piano and football."

diversion – something that draws attention away from the main action: "Daydreaming was a *diversion* from listening to the lecture." (*di-* = away)

inverse – the opposite or upside-down version: "The *inverse* of addition is subtraction." "An *inverse* image is upside down." (*in-* = in) (See Appendix C, on prefixes.)

universal – including everything: "All of the stars in the sky are the *universe*." A *universal* experience is an experience that everyone has in common. (*uni-* = one or whole)

university – an institution of higher learning that covers all fields of knowledge and may include many colleges.

reverse – to turn back. (*re-* = back)

Activities

Flip a coin and then look at the *obverse* side.

Do you have a friend who is *versatile*?

What is the *inverse* of division?

What are some *universal* things about schools?

Syllabification for correct spelling

ob-verse

88 vertigo /vur ti go /vûr' ti go'

Vertigo is often described as "dizziness." It is a condition in which the world seems to turn around or whirl. It is a serious medical symptom of some diseases, or a condition that can be induced by drugs or by rapidly turning the body in games or on amusement rides.

The previous lesson stated that the root *vers* means "turn." Both *vert* and *vers* mean "turn." Both roots come from the Latin word *vetere*, but they represent different verb forms, just like the different forms of some English verbs, such as *ran* and *ran*, or *is* and *was*.

Root
vert means "turn," as does *vers* in the previous lesson.

introvert – a person who can be described as shy, withdrawn, or not aggressive and who talks little. (*in-* = in)

extrovert – the inverse of *introvert;* an *extrovert* is outgoing, not shy, bold, and talks a lot. (*ex-* = out)

revert – to turn back: "Some people *revert* to childish ways"; "If the new system doesn't work, *revert* to the old one." (*re-* = back)

subvert – to turn over, destroy, undermine: "Don't *subvert* my intentions." (*sub-* = under)

vertex – the highest point, farthest from the base. The *vertex* of a pyramid is the point at the top, but a person's life can have a high point, or *vertex*, too.

Activities

Have you experienced *vertigo*?

Whom do you know who is an *extrovert*?

Is it always bad to *revert*?

What is the *vertex* of your life so far?

Syllabification for correct spelling

———————

ver-ti-go

An *asteroid* is a minor planet. *Asteroids* circle the sun like other planets but are much smaller, ranging in size from five hundred miles in diameter down to a fraction of a mile. There are thousands of asteroids and their average orbit radius around the sun is 2.8 astronomical units (AUs). An AU is the radius of the Earth's orbit, or about 93 million miles. So the Earth tends to be about 93 million miles from the sun, and asteroids tend to be about 260 million miles from the sun. $(93 \times 2.8 = 260)$

Root
aster or *astro* means "star."

aster – a star-shaped flower.

asterisk – a star-shaped punctuation mark (*).

astronomy – the scientific study of stars and all other heavenly bodies in the universe, such as planets and galaxies. (*-nomy* = arrangement)

astronomer – a scientist who studies astronomy. (*-er* = one who)

astrology – an ancient system of using planet positions to predict the future or to define personality types on the basis of birth date. *Astrology* is not considered valid by most astronomers but is a favorite of many newspaper column readers and fortune-tellers. Be careful not to use *astrology* when you mean *astronomy*. (*-logy* = study of)

disaster – a sudden event that causes great damage, loss, or distress. In ancient times, *disasters* were considered to be caused by the stars or foretold by astrology. (*dis-* = not)

astronaut – a crew member of a spaceship. (*naut-* = ship)

Activities

What measurement unit is used for measuring the positions of planets?

What do an *asterisk* and an *aster* flower have in common?

Does an *astrologer* study galaxies?

Is an *astronaut* related to a sailor?

Syllabification for correct spelling

as-ter-oid

As a noun, *concord* means "agreement." A *concord* can be a treaty or a formal paper of agreement. *Concord* can also have a more general meaning of acting together or acting in harmony. When capitalized, *Concord* means the capital of New Hampshire; perhaps the founders hoped that it would be a place of harmony and agreement.

In ancient times, the heart was thought to be the center of feeling or emotions and perhaps some of what we today mean by "mind." (*con-* = with)

Root
cord means "heart."

discord – lack of agreement or harmony. In music *discord* means a harsh sound. (*dis-* = not or opposite)

core – the central part of anything, such as the *core* of an apple or the *core* of an argument. In ancient times, the heart was considered the central part of the human body.

accord – to bring into agreement, to harmonize, perhaps to bring two hearts or minds together. (*ac-* = to or toward) (See Appendix C, on prefixes.)

courage – mental or moral strength or "heart": "Take *courage*, take heart; your efforts will be rewarded." (*-age* = action or process)

record – as a verb, *record* means to put in writing or perhaps some electronic form. As a noun, a *record* is the written page or perhaps an audio recording. A *record* can also be a formal history, such as a *record* of achievement or a *criminal* record. (*re-* = back)

Activities

Look to an encyclopedia for examples of political *concord*s.

What are some things that have a *core*?

Give some examples of *courage*.

Suggest some meanings for *record*.

Syllabification for correct spelling

———————————
con-cord

91 biogeography /bai oh gee og raf fee /bī' ō jē og' rə fē

Biogeography is a branch of biology that deals with the geographic distribution of plants and animals. For example, you would find tigers in Asia but not in Africa, and certain trees grow only at certain elevations. So *biogeography* is the study of life on Earth, but more literally it is a combination of geography and biology.

Root
Biogeography has three roots, or combining forms.

bio = life
geo = earth
graph = write

Here is the root *bio* in some other words:

biology – the study of life; includes many branches, such as ecology. (*-logy* = study of; related to *logic,* meaning "reason")

biography – a writing about someone else's life. (*graph* = life)

autobiography – a writing about your own life. (*auto-* = self)

biochemistry – a branch of science that combines chemistry and biology.

biopsy – the removal of tissue or fluid samples from the body for examination. (*-opsy* = vision)

antibiotic – a medicine that kills or inhibits the growth of microorganisms such as bacteria or fungi but not viruses. (*anti-* = against)

bionics – a field of study combining biology and electronics.

Activities

What are some examples of *biogeography*?

What is the difference between an *autobiography* and a *biography*?

What do doctors do during a *biopsy*?

How is *bionic* used in science fiction?

Syllabification for correct spelling
_____
bi-o-ge-og-ra-phy

A *precept* is a rule. It might be spoken, written, or simply generally understood. It could be a verbal command or a written legal order: "The general *precept* is to be cautious, but the actual law is the speed limit."

accept – to receive something with consent. You *accept* a reward or *accept* a person into your group. (*ac-* = to) (See Appendix C, on prefixes.)

Root
cept means "to take or receive."

receptacle – something that receives or holds something. A wastebasket is a *receptacle* for trash and an electric *receptacle* in the wall receives a plug. (*re-* = back; the suffix *-ical* makes it a noun)

exception – something out of the group or taken out of the norm: "Living to 107 is an *exception*. (*ex-* = from or out of)

concept – something formed in the mind. A *concept* car is formed in the mind of the designer or a sample is made, but is not yet ready for production. New *concepts* appear regularly in most fields, from architecture to dress design. (*con-* = with)

perception – an awareness of sensory information as the result of observation. *Vision* is the physical act of seeing; *perception* adds the mind in order to interpret and understand what is seen. (*per-* = through)

Activities

What are some *precepts* you know about?

What are some words that mean the opposite of *accept*?

Can you use *concept* in a sports setting?

Do you normally *see* trouble or do you *perceive* it?

Syllabification for correct spelling
_____
pre-cept

93 facilitate /fuh sill ih tate /fə sil′ i tāt′

Facilitate means to make something easier or less difficult. It might include removing impediments: "You can *facilitate* the movements of handicapped persons by putting in ramps." "Businesses are *facilitated* by less restrictive laws."

factory – a place where things are made.

Root
fac means "to do" or "to make."

manufacture – to make something. In earlier times most things were made by hand, but now *manufacturing* uses all sorts of machines. (*manu-* = hand)

fact – something already done, something that exists, an assertion that has objective reality: "The *fact* is she's tall."

benefactor – someone who does good by helping others: "The Bill and Melinda Gates Foundation is a major *benefactor* for African people with AIDS." (*bene-* = good)

malefactor – someone who does evil or is a criminal. (*male-* = bad)

facsimile – a copy of something, such as a typed page or a picture. (*sim-* = like or similar)

fax – a modern word that is a shortened version of *facsimile* (copy); usually means to send a copy by electronic means.

faculty – the teaching staff of a school, college, or university. *Faculty* is related to *facilitate,* so perhaps a *faculty's* main job is to make learning easier.

Activities

Give some instances of *facilitation*.

Does any contemporary *manufacturing* involve workers using their hands?

Name a *malefactor* mentioned in today's newspaper.

Is a photocopy a *facsimile*?

Syllabification for correct spelling

fa-cil-i-tate

An *affinity* is a liking or sympathy for or attraction to: "She had an *affinity* for dogs and old people." "Some metals have an *affinity* for chemical combination."

The first sample sentence above could be rewritten: "In the *end*, she had an *attraction* to dogs and old people." (See Appendix C, on prefixes, for an explanation of how the prefix *a-* became *af-*.)

Root
fin means "end" and *af* means "to" or "toward."

final – last. (suffix *-al* makes it an adjective)

finite – having an end or limit: "A *finite* amount is paid for that position."

infinite – having no ending, going on forever. (*in-* = not)

finicky – feeling that in the end everything must be perfect; excessively nice; too concerned: "She was a *finicky* eater and never ate bread."

confine – to keep within limits or ends: "Jails *confine* prisoners." "His illness *confines* him to a wheelchair." (*con-* = with)

definite – clear cut, having set limits or ends, leaving no doubt: "She had a *definite* goal of graduating." (The prefix *de-* has several meanings, one of which is "thoroughly.")

finish – the ending of some action: "At the *finish* of the race she came in ahead of many of the other participants"; the end coat on a polished surface: "The furniture had a fine *finish*." (*-ish* = noun)

Activities

For what do you have an *affinity*?

Name several things that are *finite*.

Identify some things that people are *finicky* about.

How can *confine* be used?

Syllabification for correct spelling
—————————
af-fin-i-ty

95 retrogress /reh truh gress /reˈ trə gresˈ

Retrogress means to go backward. Your health can make *progress* and go forward and improve, or it can *retrogress* and go backward and get worse. *Retrogress* means the same as *regress*. Both prefixes, *retro-* and *re-*, mean "back": "The chance for the new legislation to pass is *regressing*."

Root
gress means "go" or "step."

aggressive – hostile or opposing; moving strongly toward something. Someone who is *aggressive* does not step back but steps toward the enemy or vigorously attacks a situation. A person, nation, or business action can be *aggressive*. (*ag-* = to or toward) (See Appendix C, on prefixes.)

egress – to go out or a passageway for going out. An *egress* is the same as an *exit*. (*e-* = out)

ingress – to enter or an entrance; the opposite of *egress*. Lawyers talk about the "right to *ingress* and regress," which means you can both come and go, such as enter the house and leave it.

digress – to step outside the train of thought: "I *digress* from my main point for a moment." (*di-* = off; a form of the prefix *dis-*)

congress – a group of people who have come together for a specific purpose such as making laws or calling attention to a topic, such as the U.S. *Congress* or a *congress* of environmentalists. (*con-* = with or together; has the same meaning as *com-*)

Activities

Retrogress is the opposite of _____.

If you want to go out, you need to look for the _____.

Have you ever heard a speaker *digress*?

Can organizations, besides government, have a *congress*?

Syllabification for correct spelling
_____
ret-ro-gress

A *grange* is a farm and a *granger* is the farmer. In some places *farm* is by far the preferable term. However, in the U.S. Midwest, *grange* often refers to a social-business organization to which many farmers (grangers) belong.

So a farm or *grange* is primarily a place of growing seeds. After all, most of the world's population eats seeds as the main part of their diet. These include wheat, corn, rice, oats, and barley, which are from plants in the grass or monocotyledon family of plants. These seeds and the leaves of other grasses are the main food for most humans and animals, so without grass most of the world would starve to death.

Root
gran means "seed."

granola – a breakfast cereal whose main component is seeds such as oats.

granary – a place for storing grain. (*-ary* = place)

granulated – having a seedlike texture, as in "*granulated* sugar."

granite – a mineral (rock) that has the appearance of many grains or small flecks of black and white. (*-ite* = mineral)

pomegranate – a fruit whose interior is mostly seeds. (*pome-* = apple)

grain – seeds, particularly from grasses, eaten by humans and animals. *Cereal* is another word for *grain*.

ingrained – worked into the texture, either mentally or physically: "She has an *ingrained* work ethic." (*in-* = in; *-ed* = past-tense verb)

Activities

What is a *grange*?

Do you eat grass seeds?

Why is *granite* called *granite*?

What is the main ingredient of your breakfast cereal?

Syllabification for correct spelling

———————

grange

Sociability is the inclination to companionship or community life: "Man is a *sociable* animal." *Sociability* also refers to plants. For example, some pine trees group at certain elevations in the mountains, and cacti group in different environments in the desert.

Like many suffixes, however, the meaning of *-ability* is vague or not very helpful. What *is* helpful is that it changes the root into a noun form. Here are a few words that use the root *soc*:

Root

soc means "companion"; *ability* means "capacity" or "fitness."

associate – to join in a relationship; to combine; to become a partner (*as-* = to) (See Appendix C, on prefixes.)

dissociate – not to join in a relationship; to separate; to deny: "I don't like the idea so I totally *dissociate* myself from it." (*dis-* = not or opposite)

antisocial – opposed to joining with others; against society: "He is so antisocial that he won't come to the birthday party." Similar to unsociable. (*anti-* = against)

sociology – the scientific study of society, social institutions, and social relationships; can also be applied to groups of animals. (*-ology* = study of, a branch of knowledge)

socialism – a political theory or movement favoring government or collective ownership of the means of production, such as factories and farms, and the distribution of goods. It is opposed to *capitalism* or private ownership of the means of production.

socialite – a socially prominent person; someone who is active in upper society groups. (*-ite* = a person who)

Activities

Can animals have *sociability*?

From what do you *dissociate* yourself?

Name an *association*.

What is another term for capitalism?

Syllabification for correct spelling

so-cia-bil-i-ty

98 cosign /co sign /kō' sīn'

Cosigning means *signing* something along with somebody else. Be very careful about cosigning promissory notes for borrowing money, because you, as *cosigner*, are fully responsible for repaying the full amount should the original signer not pay; your credit is at risk. If you *cosign* a petition, it means that you are voting or publicly supporting an issue.

Root

sign means "mark"; *co-* means "with."

signature – your handwritten name or marking on something to signify your approval. (*-ure* = process)

assignment – task or job description. (*as-* = to) (See Appendix C, on prefixes.)

consign – not the same as cosign, c*onsign* means to transfer responsibility. A *consignee* takes items, or the *consignment,* to a shop, or to the *consignor,* to be sold. The *consignee* retains ownership until paid by the *consignor*. The suffixes *-ee* and *-or* = person; *-ee* usually indicates the person who gets the benefit—in this example, the money; and *-or* indicates the person who does the action—in this case, makes the sale and pays.

insignia – a distinguishing mark, sometimes a sign or badge of authority: "Soldiers have *insignias* for their regiment on their uniforms." (*in-* = in)

significant – having important or distinctive meaning. (*-ant* = inclined to)

Activities

Would you *cosign* a note for someone you didn't know well?

What is the difference between *cosign* and *consign*?

Can you name several *insignias*?

What does *insignificant* mean?

Syllabification for correct spelling

_____

co-sign

Purge means to "cleanse" in order to remove impurities: "If your water pipes become contaminated you must *purge* them by flushing with clean water." "The new police chief *purged* the department by removing bad officers." You can *purge* your bowels or *purge* a government.

Root
pur means "cleanse."

pure – not contaminated, not mixed with other things, without sin, clean; a correct musical note, as in a *pure tone*. You can have *pure gold* or *pure fun*.

expurgate – remove objectionable material: "Some of the movie's critics wanted the objectionable material *expurgated*." "My lawyer might want to *expurgate* a paragraph from the contract before I sign it." (*ex-* = from)

impure – not pure, contaminated, perhaps because it is not all of one substance; can also have a moral meaning: obscene, dirty, unholy. (*im-* = not)

puritan – an individual or group that has strict moral and religious beliefs and seeks to purify their souls by avoiding anything perceived as sinful. Some of the early (1600s) settlers in America were *Puritans* who left Europe so they could practice their religion in freedom.

purist – a person who is strict in following rules, particularly in the use of language.

Activities

What would you like to *purge*?

Do movie producers actually *expurgate* scenes?

Would you like to be a *puritan*?

Do you know any teachers who are *purists*?

Syllabification for correct spelling
_____
purge

100 phonetics /fon et iks   /fə net' iks

Phonetics is the scientific study of speech sounds. It is important for speech correctionists. It is also important for those who discover and try to write down previously unknown languages from such places as remote Pacific Islands and African tribes. The play *My Fair Lady* showed how Professor Higgins changed the English accent of a poor flower girl into the speech of a "lady" using his knowledge of phonetics. Higgins is a *phonetician*.

Root
phon means "sound."

The root *phon* comes from the Phoenicians, a Mediterranean people who developed the predecessor of our alphabet (a system of writing in which symbols stand for speech sounds).

telephone – an instrument for transmitting speech sounds to a distant place. (*tele-* = far)

phonics – a method of teaching beginning reading by emphasizing the sound that letters and letter patterns represent. The basic idea is to teach the student to translate the written symbols into spoken speech.

phonograph – a device for playing recorded sounds, usually music or human speech. (*graph-* = write)

phony – having false pretensions; fake, not real; all sound and no real substance. In Texas a *phony* is all hat and no cattle.

phonetic alphabet – a system of symbols for writing speech sounds that differs from and clarifies conventional spelling.

Activities

Who uses *phonetics* when discovering unknown languages?

What is a shorter word for *telephone*?

Were you given *phonics* instruction when learning to read?

Does this page have any *phonetic* alphabet on it?

Syllabification for correct spelling
_____
pho-net-ics

101 appertaining /ap per tayn ing /apˈ ər tāˈn ing

Appertaining is one of those nice old lawyer words that means simply "belonging," as in "the party of the first part shall grow into an adult with the privileges and obligations *appertaining* thereto," which means, "when he is an adult he will get the privileges and obligations that go along with it." Why don't lawyers use a word like "get" or "belong" instead of *appertain*? Maybe because it's tradition, maybe because they can charge more money for using *appertain;* in any event, knowing what *appertain* means will help if you have to read your grandfather's will. Incidentally, some modern lawyers are in favor of writing in "plain language."

Root
tain means "hold."

abstain – to hold back or refrain from doing: "Please *abstain* from smoking." (*ab-* = from)

taint – just a bit of something bad: "There was a *taint* of disgrace in her background."

contain – to hold back or down, to keep within limits; or simply to hold: "She tried to *contain* her disappointment." "What does this bottle *contain*?" (*con-* = with)

sustain – to support or continue: "How long can he *sustain* this dangerous behavior?" (*sus-*, a variant of *sub-* = under)

sustenance – something that sustains, such as food that keeps you alive.

detain – to hold back, keep from doing: "The reason she was late was that she was *detained* at school." (*de-* = from)

Activities

If Bill *appertains* the rights, who holds them?

Name some things you should *abstain* from.

What is a *container*? Name some.

What are some things that *sustain* life?

Syllabification for correct spelling

——————————

ap-per-tain-ing

The *gradient* is the amount (rate) of slope up or down in land or an object. A road and a pipeline can have a steep *gradient*. Other, nonmaterial things can have a *gradient* too; for example, when the *gradient* of music is up, the music is getting louder. Anything that has grades (steps) can have a *gradient*: a thermometer has a *gradient* in degrees.

Root
grad means "step."

grade – a step or degree used in ranking something from low to high. Schools have *grades* through which a student progresses, and class assignments can be *graded* using A,B,C, and so on or percentages.

centigrade – the grading system for temperature in the metric system of measurement, based on one hundred *gradations,* with the freezing of water occurring at zero and the boiling of water at one hundred. (*centi-* = hundred)

graduate – a person who has passed through all the grades and received a degree or a diploma; also, to receive a degree or diploma.

postgraduate – after graduation; study undertaken or degree obtained after obtaining a bachelor's degree. (*post-* = after)

gradual – proceeding by degrees or grades, little by little, slowly.

retrograde – moving backward. *Retrograde amnesia* means that the amnesia (forgetting) is getting worse. (*retro-* = back)

Activities

Name some things that have *gradients*.

Outside of school, what things have *grades*?

Are zero *centigrade* and zero Fahrenheit the same?

Is a master's degree a *postgraduate* degree?

Syllabification for correct spelling
_____
gra-di-ent

Mount has a lot of meanings, including the following:

1. to climb – to *mount* the stairs

2. to get up on – to *mount* a horse

3. to put in a position – to *mount* a statue, on a pedestal perhaps

4. to organize – to *mount* the opposition

5. to prepare – to *mount* an attack

6. to increase – to incur *mounting* costs, for example

7. shortening of "mountain" – *Mount* Rushmore.

Root

mount, as noted above, has many meanings.

paramount – higher than others, supreme: "His *paramount* purpose was to win." (*para-* = before, ahead)

surmount – to overcome, surpass: "She *surmounted* her handicap." (*sur-* = over)

tantamount – equivalent in amount or force; the same as: "The donation was *tantamount* to admitting guilt." (*tant-* ̶ so much)

mountebank – a phony or boastful pretender: Originally someone who *mounted* a bench to proclaim himself. (*-bank* = bench)

amount – to add up, be equal in value: "What does it *amount* to?" (*a-* = to)

remount – to get back up again, to *mount* again. (*re-* = back)

Activities

Use *mount* in several sentences.

What is *Paramount Pictures* trying to say about itself through its name?

Another word for *equivalent* is

_____.

Another word for *total* is

_____.

Syllabification for correct spelling

_____

mount

104 locomotion /low kuh mo shun /lō' kə mō' shən

Locomotion is the act of moving or the ability to move from place to place: "Jellyfish *locomotion* is by hydraulic propulsion (squirting water); human and dog *locomotion* is usually by walking." A *locomotive* is an engine that pulls a train from place to place.

commotion – an agitated disturbance, a hubbub, perhaps even a civil disorder. "What's all the *commotion* in the hall?" (*com-* = with)

Root
mot means "move"; *loco* means "place."

promote – to move someone or something ahead, to advance someone or something in rank. (*pro-* = forward)

emotion – feeling; mental and sometimes physical aspects of feeling; strong feeling, such as fear, anger, sorrow, and love. (*e-* is part of the prefix *ex-*, meaning "out" or "away")

remote – far away in space, time, or relation. A campground can be *remote,* or a cousin can be *remote.* (*re-* = back or away)

motive – something in a person's mind or feelings that causes him to move or act in a certain direction. (*-ive* = inclined to)

motor – a small engine, a source of mechanical power that causes movement. (*-or* = someone or something that does something)

Activities

Does a snail have *locomotion*?

A riot is a kind of _____.

Name some things that are *remote*.

Describe some *motives* you have noticed in plays or movies you have seen.

Syllabification for correct spelling
_____
lo-co-mo-tion

105 aspirate /ass pih rayt /as' pə rāt'

Aspirate is a speech sound usually represented by the letter *h*, for example, at the beginning of such words as *Harry* and *here*. It is also sometimes heard at the beginning of *wh* words, such as *when* or *while*. Note that in making the *aspirated* sound, only the *breath* is used and the vocal chords are not used. When the /h/ sound is omitted, a person's speech appears to have a dialect (as in some British dialects); it is also a characteristic of the speech of some new English speakers or some persons who have speech pronunciation problems. (*a-* = to)

The ancient Greeks equated breathing with life itself (because when you are not breathing you are not alive).

Root
spir means "breath."

expire – to die, to breathe your last breath; can also apply to inanimate subjects, for example, a lease can *expire,* or run out of life. (*ex-* = from)

perspire – to sweat (perhaps to breathe through the skin); to pass moisture through the pores of the skin or other matter, such as unglazed clay. (*per-* = through)

spirit – the principal of life that exists in any organism: "She has lost the *spirit,* or will, to keep on living"; a supernatural being, a ghost; the emotional or feeling part of the mind, as in *team spirit;* a soul or a part of God; distilled alcohol (*spirits*).

inspire – to encourage, motivate, show the way, help to become creative (*in-* – in); perhaps, "to get the *spirit* in."

Activities

List some words that have an *aspirate* sound in them.

List some things that can *expire.*

Is the moisture on a cold glass *perspiration?*

What is another name for a ghost?

Syllabification for correct spelling
———————
as-pi-rate

To *incriminate* is to charge with a crime or to furnish evidence that shows guilt: "Don't *incriminate* him until you have more evidence."

crime – an extreme violation of the law: "Murder and theft are *crimes*, a traffic violation is not a *crime*."

criminology – the scientific study of crime and criminals. (*-ology* = study of)

criminologist – one who studies crime. (*-ist* = one who)

Root
crim means "crime" and sometimes "accuse."

discriminate – to find the differences between things or people: "It is good to *discriminate* between acts of generosity and acts of greed; it is bad to *discriminate* between people of different skin colors for the purpose of predicting failure." (*dis-* = from, apart)

indiscriminate – not discriminate: "She was *indiscriminate* in her TV viewing and watched a lot of junk as well as good things." (*in-* = not)

recriminate – to make a counter accusation: "When she charged him with lying, he *recriminated* and said that *she* was lying." (*re-* = back, again)

Activities

Who usually does the *incriminating* in our society?

What other "ologies" might study crime?

Is it all right to *discriminate* in liking kinds of music?

Is it common for a criminal to *recriminate*?

Syllabification for correct spelling
_____
in-crim-i-nate

A *curator* is one who cares for, or supervises, a museum or library: "There is a special *curator* for the stamp collection." A *curator* can also be the guardian of a minor child: "A *curator* for James was appointed by the court."

curate – an assistant to a clergyman.

Root
cur means "care."

cure – to heal something, to give medical assistance: "Antibiotics can *cure* an infection"; to preserve meats, as in *sugar-cured ham.*

curious – interested in learning about something: "He was *curious* about the strange noise."

accurate – careful, striving for no errors. (*ac-* = to) (See Appendix C, on prefixes.)

sinecure /sin ih kyur/ – a job that pays well without much work. (*sine-* = without; hence, "a job without cares")

secure – safe, without cares: "Keep your money in a *secure* place so it won't get lost or stolen." (*se-* = without)

insecure – feeling uncertain or fearful; lacking confidence; not fastened properly. (*in-* = not)

procure – to obtain something: "The quartermaster *procured* food for the troops." (*pro-* = for)

Activities

Where is a *curator* likely to work?

Who employs a *curate*?

Is *curiosity* a good thing for a student?

Would you like to have a *sinecure*?

Syllabification for correct spelling
_____
cu-ra-tor

Obdurate means to persist stubbornly in wrongdoing, resist persuasion: "No matter how much he learned, he was *obdurate* about continuing to smoke."

   Obdurate is not hard like hitting a cement floor, but hard like resisting change or lasting a long time.

> **durable** – lasting a long time despite frequent use: "Levi's jeans are *durable*." (-*able* = is, can be)

> **endure** – to continue in the same way, to put up with hardship, to remain firm despite the circumstances: "She *endured* the pain because she still had miles to hike; she had *endurance*." (*en-* = in) (See Appendix C, on prefixes.)

> **duress** – pressure by force; restraint: "He was under *duress* to get better grades." (-*ess* = noun form)

> **duration** – the period for which something lasts: "They enlisted for the *duration* of the war."

Root
dur means "hard" or "lasting."

unendurable – incapable of being continued or handled any longer. (*un-* = not)

during – at some point in period continuing action: "He fell asleep *during* the lesson." (-*ing* = continuing action)

Activities

Are repeat criminals *obdurate*?

Name some *durable* things.

What do you have to *endure*?

Do football games have a *duration*?

Syllabification for correct spelling

_____

ob-du-rate

A *presentiment* is a feeling that something is about to happen. When it's a feeling that something bad will happen, it could be called a *foreboding;* if it is just that anything, good or bad, is about to happen, it could be called a *premonition.* A *presentiment* is not based on a previously known fact or outside information but rather is a vague feeling or strong direct perception: "I had a *presentiment* that you would call."

Root
sent means "feeling."

absent – missing; not here at the present time. (*ab-* = from)

essence – the basic, underlying characteristic or element of something: "The *essence* of . . . is. . . ." "Politeness is *essential* when meeting a stranger." *Essence* can also be another word for *perfume,* which some women think is *essential.*

quintessential – the purest, most typical, most characteristic, most basic form of something: "She was the *quintessential* movie star." (*quint-* = fifth)

A *heterophone* is a word that is spelled the same but has a different pronunciation and meaning, as in:

pre' sent – a gift (noun).

pre sent' – to introduce, to bring forth a charge or evidence (verb): "Please *present* the new pupil to the principal."

Activities

Have you or a friend ever had a *presentiment?*

Describe some *essences.*

Now describe some *quintessentials.*

Use the two different pronunciations of *present* in a sentence.

Syllabification for correct spelling

pre-sen-ti-ment

Fixate means to focus your gaze and your attention on something without wavering or changing: "She was *fixated* on the snake crawling into the room through a hole in the floor."

Root
fix actually means "to fix" and has several uses.

1. to repair or correct something: "*Fix* the broken door."

2. an embarrassing or difficult position: "She was in a *fix*."

3. take a bribe or favor: "In exchange for a date he agreed to *fix* her traffic ticket."

4. to attach: "She used double-sided tape to *fix* the picture to the wall."

5. to stop change: "I'll *fix* that situation permanently."

fix appears in such words as:

fixture – something put in place permanently: "The cabinet was a *fixture* on the wall." "The old man was a *fixture* on the park bench; he came every day to sit there."

prefix – a syllable fixed at the front of a word. (*pre-* = before)

suffix – a syllable fixed at the end of a word. (*suf-* = under or below) (See prefix *sub-* in Appendix C.)

affix – to attach; a syllable inserted at the beginning or end of a word to produce a derivative. (*af-* = to) (See prefix *ad-* in Appendix C.)

infix – an affix (syllable) placed in the middle of a word; for example, the *for-* in *unforgiving*.

crucifix – a cross on which people in ancient times were hanged as a means of execution; also used as a religious symbol. (*cruci-* = cross)

Activities

Did you ever see a cat *fixate* on a mouse?
What *fixtures* do you have in your house?
Is a *suffix* an *affix*?
What does *crucify* mean?

Syllabification for correct spelling
_____
fix-ate

111 crony /kro nee /krō' nē

A *crony* is a close companion, someone you have known for a long time. Supposedly originating in the seventeenth century as a slang word from Cambridge University, it has come to be recognized as a full-fledged English word, which illustrates that slang can be adopted into standard use. Most slang words do not become regular words, however, at least as evidenced by their lack of inclusion in a regular dictionary; slang words change or quickly drop out of use. There are specialized slang dictionaries. *Crony* can also be correctly spelled *chrony*.

Root
cron or *chron*
means "time."

cronyism – the unsavory practice of appointing one's friends, or *cronies,* to important positions. It's not a new idea; a more classical word for the same practice is *nepotism.*

anachronism – a person or event appearing in the wrong time frame: "Driving a horse and buggy is an *anachronism* in the twenty-first century."

chronometer – a device for measuring time. A watch could be called a *chronometer,* but usually a *chronometer* is a more sensitive, accurate, and specialized instrument. Races are timed by *chronometers,* ships navigate using *chronometers.* (*meter* = measure)

synchronized – scheduled to occur simultaneously or occurring at the same time: "In gas engines the spark must be *synchronized* with the position of the piston." "In *synchronized* swimming all the swimmers do the same movements together or at the same time." (*syn-* = with)

Activities

Do you have some *cronies*?

Name some *anachronisms*.

What do *chronometers* do?

Name several events that need to be *synchronized*.

Syllabification for correct spelling
_____
cro-ny

Assonance is a poetry term meaning that the vowel sounds in nearby words rhyme, that is, are the same. It's not the whole syllable that rhymes, just the vowel or vowels, as in *queen* and *leap*, and *bike* and *time*. Examples of regular rhyme, by contrast, include *feed* and *plead*, and *beam* and *team*. Many slang phrases or clichés have *assonance*, for example, "give me a high five," "free as a breeze," and "mad as a hatter." The prefix *as-* means "to."

Root
son means "sound."

sonic – the speed of sound. At sea level, the speed of sound is 738 miles per hour. In a different context, *sonic* also means having a frequency that can be heard by the human ear, or about 20 to 20,000 cycles per second.

supersonic – faster than the speed of sound: "Some military jets are *supersonic*." (*super-* = over)

subsonic – below the speed of sound: "Most commercial planes are *subsonic*." (*sub-* = under)

transonic – between subsonic and supersonic (the speed of sound varies with altitude and weather conditions). (*trans-* = across)

dissonant – making a harsh, clashing noise, like a band or orchestra tuning up, or two people yelling at each other. (*dis-* = opposite)

sonata – a musical composition for one or two instruments in three or four movements.

Activities

Can you think of some clichés or make up some slang that uses *assonance*?

Can a frequency of 10,000 cycles per second be heard by a human?

What vehicles can be *supersonic*?

Is a *sonata dissonant*?

Syllabification for correct spelling
—————————————
as-so-nance

Insolvent means that you are broke, bankrupt, unable to pay your bills, or as a banker might say, have no liquidity. It is a rather polite way of saying you have no cash.

So *insolvent* literally means "not loose"—financially you are not loose.

solvent – means you do have money and are able to pay your debts. A *solvent* is also a liquid used for dissolving or loosening things: "Water is a *solvent* for sugar, and paint thinner is a *solvent* for grease."

Root

solv and *solu* mean "to loosen," *in-* means "not," *-ent* means "inclined to."

dissolve and **dissolution** – to loosen, disburse: "Divorce is the *dissolution* of a marriage." "Legal partnerships can *dissolve* and the partners separate." "Large companies can *dissolve* into smaller units or companies." (*de-* = from)

resolve – to break up: "A beam of white light can be *resolved* into a rainbow of colors by passing through a prism." "A problem can be *resolved* (or broken up) by a *resolution*, or formal agreement." *Resolve* can also mean a "fixed purpose": "He had the *resolve* to do better next time." (*re-* = back)

irresolute – wishy-washy, faint-hearted, infirm, indecisive, "someone who just can't make up his mind." (*ir-* = not)

Activities

Have there been times when you have been *insolvent*?

What is the opposite of *insolvent*?

What are the two opposite meanings that *resolve* seems to have?

Are we all *irresolute* sometimes?

Syllabification for correct spelling

———————————
in-sol-vent

114 discipline /dis suh plin /dis' ə plin

Discipline has several meanings, all centered around the idea of learning:

1. *Discipline* is training that corrects or improves the mind or character: "Learning to play the piano or learning to spell requires some *discipline*."

2. *Discipline* is a subject that is taught or a branch of knowledge: "The *discipline* of physics requires a good knowledge of mathematics."

3. *Discipline* is punishment: "We *discipline* our dog by saying 'No!' forcefully."

4. *Discipline* is control or restraint: "Members of the police department must have the *discipline* not to make unnecessary arrests."

Root
disci means "learn."

disciplinarian – an authoritarian or taskmaster; one who strictly enforces the rules: "An army drill sergeant is the ultimate *disciplinarian*."

self-discipline – learning on your own or restraining yourself from engaging in bad behavior, without outside force: "She really has *self-discipline*! She learned to read Latin all on her own."

undisciplined – the opposite of self-disciplined: "He is *undisciplined* and won't stop smoking."

disciple – someone who follows or learns from a leader or master of a subject: "The apostles were *disciples* of Jesus."

Activities

Can a teacher of mathematics have *disciples*?

Does a school need to *discipline* its students?

What are some things that require *self-discipline*?

Are drug addicts *undisciplined*?

Syllabification for correct spelling
_____
dis-ci-pline

Tort is a legal term that means a legal wrong for which somebody can be sued. Because such a wrong is not necessarily a crime, or at least not a major crime, the public prosecutor might not bring criminal action; nevertheless, it is a violation of a person's rights and the violator (individual or company) can be sued in a civil action. Not paying a bill or not living up to a contract can be a tort.

Incidentally, a *torte* is a cake.

Root
tort, or simply *tor,* means "twist."

torch – a stick, originally made with twisted grass or other material, that is soaked with resin or gasoline, then set afire and used for light. In modern England a *torch* is an electric flashlight.

torture – the infliction or experience of extreme pain. A bad headache can *torture* you, but so can an enemy inflict *torture* on you for the purpose of trying to get you to tell the truth or for punishment.

contor- tionist – a person who can twist his body into strange and extreme positions. (*con-* = with)

contorted – twisted, knotted, or all tangled up: a pile of string, a body, or a political argument can be *contorted.*

extortion – an attempt to extract money or information from someone who doesn't want to give it. An *extortionist* might twist your arm or apply another kind of pressure.

torque – rotational pressure (rather than straight pressure such as gravity or pushing). *Torque* is caused by a spinning or rotating force such as an electric motor or a wrench turning a bolt.

Activities

Can you name any *torts*?

What are some *torture* techniques?

Describe some *contorted* reasoning.

What is the difference between *influence* and *extortion*?

Syllabification for correct spelling

_____

tort

Atonement is something you do to make up for having done something wrong; it is a reparation for an offense or injury: "He had her whole car painted in *atonement* for smashing her rear fender."

When the root *tone* is used in modern words, however, it takes on some interesting variations in meaning:

Root
tone or *ton*
means "tone,"
as you might
expect.

monotonous – boring, tiring, unchanging, like a musical piece or speech expressed in only one tone or note. (*mono-* = one)

detonate – set off an explosive; make a loud sound like thunder. (*de-* = from)

halftone – the shades of gray between the darkest and lightest parts of a photograph.

atonal – a type of modern music that avoids traditional tonality; to some it sounds strange or like cacophony. (*a-* = without)

tonic – a drink, medicine, or activity that you use to tone yourself up.

intone – in music, to use long, sustained tones; in speech, to talk in tones that sound like singing, such as in reciting prayers or poems.

undertone – soft speech or a meaning that is not obvious: "The *undertone* of the meeting was hostility."

Activities

Have you ever made an *atonement*?

Have you ever been in a *monotonous* class?

Try reading a poem with heavy *intonation*.

Is it important to recognize *undertones*?

Syllabification for correct spelling
————————————
a-tone-ment

An *investiture* is a formal ceremony to install a person into a high position such as a judgeship, a university presidency, a church office, or the presidency of an organization. Literally it means putting on the robes of office. In the Middle Ages, the robes or clothes you wore identified the trade or profession to which you belonged.

vest – a sleeveless, close-fitting garment usually worn under a coat.

Root
vest means "garment."

vestments – garments worn by clergy, such as the cassock, a long gown. Three hundred years ago what we now call a cassock was called a vest.

investment – money put into a business to give the investor part ownership. The *investment* may be used to cover startup or expansion costs. (*in-* = in)

vested – having ownership or rights: "Her pension money is *vested;* it's hers even if she quits her job."

divestment – taking money out of a business. (*di-* = twice)

reinvest – to put money back into a business. (*re-* = back)

transvestite – someone who wears clothes usually worn by the opposite sex; a *cross-dresser*. (*trans-* = across)

travesty – a sham, parody, or cruel joke: "The way she treats her children is a *travesty*." (*tra-* = across)

Activities

Have you ever heard about or attended an *investiture*?

Describe a *vest*.

What are some *investments* shown in the newspaper?

Can you recognize a *transvestite* if you see one?

Syllabification for correct spelling

———————————

in-ves-ti-ture

Variegated often refers to the multicolored leaves of a plant. The leaves of most plants are one color (green), but some plants naturally or by special breeding have leaves that are green intermixed with white or other colors. *Variegated* can also apply to anything with a mixture or dappling of colors, from women's clothing to the fur of spider monkeys.

Root
vari means "changeable," "diverse," or "speckled."

variety – numerous forms or types, an assortment of choices, or a subspecies: "That's a different *variety* of flower." "I like a *variety* of boyfriends."

variant – something that is different from normal: "That bird with the unusual white spot is a *variant*."

variance – a degree of difference: "One or two degrees of *variance* is still normal"; a permitted variation from the rule: "They need a *variance* from the planning board so they can build their house nearer the street than what is normally permitted."

variable – changing or unpredictable: "Her opinions were so *variable* that they changed from day to day."

vary – to bring about change: "His routine did not *vary* from day to day." A similar but unrelated word, *very*, is an intensifier: "She is *very* happy"; it comes from a root meaning "true."

Activities

Have you seen a plant with *variegated* leaves?

Name some things that have different *varieties*.

How much *variance* is allowed in following speed laws?

What is the difference between *vary* and *very*?

Syllabification for correct spelling
———————————
var-i-e-gat-ed

Awkward means "clumsy" or "lacking in physical coordination": "He was so *awkward* that he spilled everything." *Awkward* can also apply to social situations that do not go smoothly: "She felt *awkward* when she had to decline to dance."

backward	forward	downward
northward	eastward	upward
wayward	inward	outward

Root
ward means "direction."

The prefix *awk-* means "wrong," so someone who is *awkward* is moving in the wrong direction. There is another possible origin, however: the Middle English meaning of *awk-* is "left-handed." Because the majority of people are right-handed, their left hand is less skillful or, you might say, *awkward*. The word *gauche* /go sh/, taken from the French, means "socially *awkward*," and in French it also means "left."

The root *ward* can also mean "guard," as in:

warden – an official charged with guarding or supervising, such as a *game warden* or the *warden of a prison*.

reward – something given in appreciation for good or evil done; related to showing your appreciation.

ward – a person who is guarded, such as a *ward of the court*; the action of guarding: to "*ward off* the enemy"; a politically defined geographic area: "The city is divided into twelve *wards*."

Activities

Describe an *awkward* situation.
What are some words using the root *ward* to mean direction?
What are some kinds of *rewards*?
Which meaning of *ward* is in "hospital ward" or "city ward"?

Syllabification for correct spelling

awk-ward

Ultrasound is sound beyond the upper limit of human hearing, which is about 20,000 cycles per second, so humans cannot hear these sounds. Some animals, such as dogs and bats, can hear in the range above the human level.

ultimate – the highest possible, beyond anything normal or usual: "Winning the Super Bowl was the *ultimate* joy."

Prefix *ultra-* means "beyond."

penultimate – next to the last: "Chapter 29 is the *penultimate* chapter in a 30-chapter book." (*pen-* = almost)

antepenultimate – preceding the next to last (*ante-* = before)

ultimatum – final demand or proposal: "The strikers gave an *ultimatum:* Sign the contract or we won't work tomorrow."

ultramicro – very small. *Microscopic* means that something is so small you can see it only with a microscope; *ultramicro* (short for *ultramicroscopic*) means smaller than that: "An atom is *ultramicro*."

The prefix *ultra-*, meaning "beyond," is seen in numerous compound words, such as:

ultraconservative	ultraliberal	ultraheavy
ultramilitant	ultranationalist	ultrahot
ultramodern	ultraorthodox	ultrarealism

Activities

Have you ever heard a dog bark at something you can't hear?

What is your *ultimate* joy?

What is the *penultimate* lesson in this book?

Have you heard someone give an *ultimatum*?

Syllabification for correct spelling

ul-tra-sound

121 mortified /mor tih fide /môr' tə fīd'

Mortified means "embarrassed to death." Well, maybe not really to death, but pretty badly: "When her dress ripped on stage she was *mortified.*" *Mortified* can also have another, sort of deadly aspect in that a wound that is gangrenous (infected) is called *mortifying.*

immortal – something that will never die: "Truth is *immortal.*" (*im-* = not)

Root
mort means "death."

mortal – something that will die: "All humans are *mortal.*" Also, a *mortal* is a human being.

mortician – a person who takes care of dead bodies and conducts funerals and burials.

mortuary – a place where a mortician works.

mortgage – a pledge or lien on a property as security for the repayment of money borrowed. In France it used to be considered a "dead pledge," so no matter whether the borrower died, the *mortgage* was still on the property.

amortize – to pay part of the principal of a loan or mortgage over a time until it is paid off; to write off the cost of an asset over time. (*a-* = to)

postmortem – occurring after death, such as an autopsy or the rehashing of a lost football game. (*post-* = after)

Activities

When have you been *mortified*?

Identify some things that are *immortal.*

When buying a house, most people need a _____.

The discussion of a play that died on opening night is called a _____.

Syllabification for correct spelling

_____

mor-ti-fied

122 journalistic /jur nal iss tick /jûr' nl is' tik

Journalistic means written in the style of newspapers: "The short story was not written in traditional prose style but instead was more *journalistic*." Newspaper articles traditionally answered the five Ws: who, what, why, when, where, and how, but this form isn't always followed exactly. What *journalistic* writing is supposed to do is be factual, free of opinion, and free of the use of personal pronouns.

Root
journ
means "daily."

journal – a daily record. Accountants keep a *journal* of financial transactions. Writers keep a *journal* of their daily thoughts or happenings. The word *journal* is also commonly used as part of the name of newspapers.

journey – a trip of any length, although it originally meant one day's travel. *Journey* may also be used metaphorically to mean "passage," as in "life's *journey*."

journalism – broadly speaking, the collection, writing, editing, and publishing of information in newspapers and other media, including television, radio, and magazines.

journeyman – originally meant a person who worked for another person by the day. The word has evolved to mean someone who is skilled and experienced at a craft or trade, such as plumbing or carpentry. *Journeyman* is a stage of skill higher than *apprentice* but lower than *master*.

Activities

Describe characteristics of the *journalistic* style of writing in your newspaper.

Do you keep a *journal*? It's not a bad idea.

How long can a *journey* be?

What crafts have *journeymen*?

Syllabification for correct spelling
_____
jour-nal-is-tic

Maritime has to do with commerce or navigation of the sea, so it refers to the commercial shipping industry and to land regions near the sea: "Canada has *maritime* provinces next to the Atlantic Ocean." "*Maritime law* are laws pertaining to ships."

mariner – a seaman, sailor, or anyone who goes to the sea to make a living or helps to navigate or operate ships.

Root
mari means "sea."

submarine – a ship that goes beneath the surface of the sea. *Submarine* can also refer to anything below the surface of the ocean: "*Submarines* have instruments for taking the sea's temperature." "*Submarine* plants grow only below the ocean's surface." (*sub-* = under)

marine – nearly anything related to the sea, as in *marine environment*. When capitalized, *Marine* refers to a person who is a member of the *Marine Corps*, an armed force of soldiers originally under the supervision of the Navy and stationed aboard ships.

aquamarine – a gemstone that is *marine* or sea colored, frequently light blue. (*aqua-* = water)

merchant marine – the commercial shipping industry and its personnel; privately owned commercial ships, as distinguished from the Navy.

Activities

Two words that generally relate to the sea are _____ and _____.

Vessels and plants under the sea are _____.

A sea-colored gemstone is an _____.

A large ship is usually part of the Navy or the _____.

Syllabification for correct spelling
_____
mar-i-time

Formalism is excessive concern with forms, rules, or rituals that deemphasizes content: "Her pictures had plenty of *formalistic* style but little meaning." "The king's court had rigid *formalism* and no power." "The new religious service decreased the *formalism* and increased the spirit."

Root
form means "shape."

formal – having fixed rules, customs, or shape, as in *formal dress, formal ceremony,* and *formal greeting.*

conform – to take on the same shape, outline, or contour: "The house *conformed* with the others on the block." *Conform* can also mean to comply or be in harmony with: "Hippies don't want to *conform* with the standards of the community." (*con-* = with)

nonconforming – the opposite of conforming. (*non-* = not)

perform – to carry out or complete: "He won't *perform* his part of the contract"; to participate in a play or to act in front of an audience. (*per-* = through)

reform – to make better by correcting faults or defects; to restore to a former good state. "Prisons try to *reform* criminals." (*re-* = back)

uniform – always having the same shape, clothes, color, and so on: "Soldiers have *uniform* rifles." (*uni-* = one)

format – the makeup of a book, including shape, typeface, size, and so on. Can also apply to plans for action, such as the *format* of a TV show.

Activities

Is *formalism* good or bad?

Is it good or bad to *conform*?

In addition to a play, how else could someone *perform*?

Describe a *format* for a meeting or TV show.

Syllabification for correct spelling

for-mal-ism

Anything *frangible* is easily broken. Certainly an egg shell is *frangible*, but *frangible* is also often used in more esoteric descriptions, such as: "Her dainty nose was pink and *frangible*," and in business: "Don't ship in *frangible* containers."

Root words sometimes have more than one spelling. In this case, the roots *frag* and *fract* both mean "break." Both spellings come from the same Latin word but represent different parts of speech.

Root

frang means "break"; *-ible* means "able."

fracture – anything that is broken, especially a bone or a relationship. A *crack* is sometimes referred to as a *fracture*.

fractious – unruly or causing trouble; quarrelsome; not smooth. All sorts of things can be *fractious*: a teenager, a horse, a crowd of protesters.

fraction – part of a whole. In mathematics there is the *common fraction* (such as 3/4) and the *decimal fraction* (such as 1.75). In more general use, a *fraction* is a small part: "He got only a *fraction* of the votes needed to win."

infraction – a breaking or violation of rules or a treaty: "Talking at the wrong time in class is an *infraction*." It can also be a broken bone in which the broken portions do not separate—an incomplete fracture.

Activities

Name some things that are *frangible*.

Describe a *fractious* person or situation.

What are some *infractions*?

What kind of a *fraction* is 1/2?

Syllabification for correct spelling

---
fran-gi-ble

126 circuitous /sir kyoo i tuss /sər kyōō' i təs

Circuitous means moving in a roundabout manner rather than in a direct line, or "going in circles": "Rivers can be *circuitous* and end up not far from where they started." "Arguments can proceed in a *circuitous* manner so that it is hard to see how they are getting anywhere."

circus – a show featuring animal acts and acrobats that is usually held in a ring or large circle.

Root
circ means "ring" or "around."

circuit – a more or less circular path; often a work-related route with periodic stops, such as a mail route. Also a chain of theaters that take turns hosting the performance of a play that moves from theater to theater on the *circuit*. An *electrical circuit* carries electric power to various outlets. A *circuit court* originally moved from town to town, but now it serves a particular geographic area.

circumference – the distance around something: "The *circumference* of a building is the sum of the distance of each side." (*fer* = carry)

circulate – to move around: "The hostess liked to *circulate* at her large parties so that she could meet everybody."

semicircle – a half circle. (*semi-* = half)

encircle – to enclose in a circle: "During the battle the Confederates *encircled* the Union soldiers." (*en-* = in)

Activities

Would you trust a *circuitous* used-car salesman?

What are some uses for the word *circuit*?

If you know the radius, how can you find the *circumference* of a circle?

What does "*circulate* a memorandum" mean?

> **Syllabification for correct spelling**
> _____
> **cir-cu-i-tous**

A *royalty* is a tax or a percentage of money received in exchange for a right. For example, a book author receives a *royalty*, or percentage of the income, for giving the publisher the right to publish and sell his or her book. A *royalty* can also be based on a patent, or on mineral rights, such as oil *royalties* that are paid to the landowner for granting the right to extract oil. Originally *royalties* were a tax paid to the king; the king had a right to them because he needed the money to run the government, conduct wars, and have a few banquets.

Root
roy and *rag* mean "king," but their usage is much broader.

Royalty also refers to persons related to the king, such as princes and other members of the royal family. Historically the king was the government as well as at the top of the social structure.

royalist – someone who supports the king.

viceroy – a person who rules an area in the king's name; the governor of a province: "India was ruled by a *viceroy* when it was part of the British Empire." The prefix *vice-* means "one who takes the place of" or "assistant," as in *vice principal*, *vice president*, and *vice-consul*.

regal – kingly: "To wear *regal* attire is to dress like a king."

regalia – ceremonial dress or insignias (badges or other distinguishing marks) suitable for wearing to the king's court or to other high occasions.

Regina – a female name meaning "queen." (*Rex* is a male name meaning "king.")

Activities

Is there any difference between a *royalty* and a tax?

Are there still *royalists* in Britain?

What does a *viceroy* do?

Can an ordinary person act in a *regal* manner?

Syllabification for correct spelling

---

roy-al-ty

A *tribute* is money or something else valuable paid from one nation to another as acknowledgment of submission: "When the Roman army conquered a smaller nation, the smaller nation was forced to pay an annual *tribute*." A *tribute* is like a tax, only larger. In more recent times, *tribute* has come to mean voluntary honor, praise, or recognition of service paid to a person or organization: "They gave the retiring teacher a luncheon as a *tribute* for her 50 years of service."

Root
tribute
means "give."

tributary – the money paid as part of a *tribute*; also a small stream or river that flows into a larger stream, river, or lake.

contribute – to give in common with others: "You should *contribute* to the Red Cross." "I hope you will *contribute* your ideas to the discussion." (*con-* = with)

distribute – to hand out or divide among many: "The community members joined to *distribute* food to the disaster victims." Other things that can be *distributed* include charm, grass seed, land (to heirs), and work to be done. (*dis-* = apart, pieces)

attribute – a characteristic or aspect of a person's character: "She has the pleasing *attribute* of being happy most of the time." *Attribute*, used as a verb, also means to declare the cause of something: "He *attributed* his success to hard work." (*at-* = to)

Activities

Have you participated in a *tribute*?

Where is there a *tributary* stream near you?

To what have you made a contribution?

Name one *attribute* of a family member.

Syllabification for correct spelling
_____
trib-ute

A *similitude* is a close likeness. A person who is a *similitude* may be called a double, counterpart, or resemblance: "Her new friend was a haunting *similitude*."

similar – resembling something but not exactly the same: "His new house is *similar* to the last one."

Root
simi means
"like."

dissimilar – not similar: "After two months he still hadn't adjusted to his *dissimilar* surroundings." (*dis-* = apart or opposite)

simulate – to give a similar appearance of something; to fake, not be real or original: "Her singing could only *simulate* the tone of the rock star."

facsimile – a copy or likeness: "The picture he bought was a *facsimile*, not an original"; shortened to *fax* in modern offices: "Send the completed document to her via the *fax* machine." (*fac* = do or make)

assimilate – to take in or absorb: "She could hardly *assimilate* all the new information she got from the lecture."

simile – a figure of speech that compares two things using *like* or *as:* "She was as pretty as a new rose." Similar to *metaphor,* which uses a word or phrase to mean something else and is often used in poetry and fiction: "She is a rose like no other." Note: *like* and *as* are not used in most metaphors.

Activities

Do you know anybody who is a *similitude* of a TV star?

What is the difference between *similar* and *similitude*?

Do you have trouble *assimilating* something new?

Make up several *similes*.

Syllabification for correct spelling
_____
si-mil-i-tude

Multifarious means having great variety: "The farmer's wife must carry out *multifarious* activities, from raising corn to raising children."

multiply – to increase greatly: "The number of readers is *multiplied* by the availability of free libraries"; in mathematics, to increase a number by adding the number to itself a number of times: "*Multiplying* 2 by 3 means adding 2 to itself 3 times, or $2 \times 3 = 6$."

Prefix *multi* means "many"; *farious* means "ways" or "sides."

multilateral – having many sides: "In *multilateral* talks, more than two sides or nations talk and negotiate." (*lateral-* = side)

multitude – a large number of persons or things: "The prophet spoke to a *multitude*." "I have a *multitude* of things to do before I go."

multiplicity – a large number of things; not used for people, yet both *multiplicity* and *multitude* can be used for actions and things: "It is hard to understand the universe because of the *multiplicity* of factors affecting it." (*pli-* = folds or layers)

multiform – having many forms or shapes: "Ghosts and goblins are *multiform* depending on the imaginations of the authors of the stories told about them." (*form* = form)

Activities

What occupations involve *multifarious* activities?

Is a football game *multilateral*?

What is the difference between *multitude* and *multiplicity*?

What is the difference between *multiform* and *uniform*?

Syllabification for correct spelling

---

mul-ti-far-i-ous

Flamboyant means flaming, showy, ornate. *Flamboyant* frequently refers to a speech or speaker who uses colorful phrases and a lively animated style. It can also refer to advertisements or to a style of dressing or decorating: "Her dress was too *flamboyant* to wear to class." And it can refer to a style of architecture that uses a lot of wavy lines, suggestive of flames.

Root
flam or *flag*
means
"fire."

flame – the glowing part of a fire; created by igniting gas; gives off light and heat due to the combining of the gas with oxygen in the air.

inflame – to set on fire; usually used metaphorically to mean to get someone excited about something: "He was *inflamed* by the remark about his school."

inflammatory – inflamed or excited; frequently applied to a speech that arouses anger or to hostility expressed toward the government or an enemy.

flamingo – a bird with flaming pink or reddish feathers.

conflagration – a fire, frequently large and disastrous: "The whole city was destroyed in the *conflagration*." (*con-* – with)

flagrant – extreme, outstanding, purposeful; often used in the sense of bad or notorious: "He demonstrated a *flagrant* disregard for the law."

Activities

Describe any *flamboyant* hairstyles you have seen.

Should you be careful about responding to people who make *inflammatory* speeches?

Is *flagrant* closely related in meaning to *conflagration*?

Have you ever seen a *flamingo*?

Syllabification for correct spelling

---

flam-boy-ant

A *pendulum* is a weight that hangs on a cord or an arm so it can swing freely back and forth. Once the *pendulum* is set in motion, it continues to swing back and forth because of gravity, until it runs out of energy. *Pendulums* are found in old-fashioned clocks, where they regulate the time-keeping mechanism. *Foucault pendulums* are the huge, very heavy *pendulums* with long (20- to 30-foot) arms that are seen in museums. They demonstrate the Earth's rotation.

Pendulum can also refer to any object or person that swings from side to side.

Root
pend means "hang."

pendulous – swinging like a *pendulum*. A vine hanging from a tree or a monkey hanging by one arm can be *pendulous*.

pending – not decided; continuing: "She has a *pending* court case; it might be decided next month."

pendant – something that is hanging: "Women often wear a piece of jewelry called a *pendant* around their neck." Ornaments hanging from a chandelier can also be called *pendants*.

pennant – a flag shaped like a triangle that usually hangs from a pole or rope.

Activities

Make a *pendulum* with a string and a rock.

Name something that is *pending*.

Draw a picture of a *pennant*.

Find someone who is wearing a *pendant*.

Syllabification for correct spelling
_____
pen-du-lum

A *micron* (also called a *micrometer*) is an extremely small unit of measurement—one thousandth of a millimeter—and a millimeter is one thousandth of a meter. Thus a meter, which is about three feet, can be broken down into tinier and tinier units:

centimeter, one hundredth of a meter = .39 inch

> *millimeter,* one thousandth of a meter = .039 inch

> *micrometer,* one thousandth of a millimeter =.000039 inch

Prefix
micro- means "small."

Modern scientists are now working in *nanometers,* which are one billionth of a meter, or 10^{-9} (ten to the minus 9th power). *Nanotechnology* is technology such as making electronic circuits using switches so small that they are measured in *nanometers*.

microcosm – a tiny world or miniature universe; a sample of a larger universe: "An atom is a *microcosm* of a solar system." "A school can be a *microcosm* of the real world." (*cosmo-* = universe)

microscope – an instrument for viewing very small things. (*scope* = view)

microbe – a very small organism, such as a bacterium.

microorganism – the same thing as a *microbe*.

microwave – a very short electromagnetic wave between 1 centimeter and 100 centimeters in length. *Microwave* may also mean a device that uses *microwaves* to heat food.

Activities

What is another name for a *micrometer*?

How big is a *micron* in inches?

Can you think of any *microcosms*?

Do you have any *microbes* in you?

How did *microwave oven* get its name?

Syllabification for correct spelling

_____

mi-cron

Candor is the quality of being open, honest, and frank: "You can depend on her *candor* and complete honesty."

candle – usually a round column of wax with a wick in the middle that is set afire to give off light. *Candle* is also a unit used to measure light (luminous intensity), also called an *international candle*. Used as a verb, *candle* means to hold an egg so a strong light shining through it will show imperfections within the egg.

Root
cand means "white" but can also imply "light" or "shining."

candid – the adjective form of *candor:* "He held to his *candid* opinion."

candidate – someone seeking public office, an employment position, or membership in a selective group. In ancient Rome, a *candidate* wore a white gown.

incandescent – a white surface so bright it seems to be glowing, radiant, clear, and brilliant: "Her sheets were so clean they were *incandescent*." "Light bulbs are *incandescent* when turned on." (*-escense* = action)

candelabrum or **candelabra** – a large standing holder for a candle or many candles; should not be used as a synonym for *chandelier,* which hangs from the ceiling.

Activities

Do you want a friend to have *candor*?

Can you name any current *candidates*?

Is a *candid* opinion good or bad?

What is the difference between a *candelabra* and a *chandelier*?

Syllabification for correct spelling
_____
can-dor

Minutia is a very small thing, a small detail, or a petty matter. The plural of minutia is *minutiae:* "She was caught up in all the details and *minutiae* of the job." "Don't bother me with *minutiae*, I'm too busy."

minimum – the smallest possible amount, the least action, the lowest quality, the least permissible: "He wants to do the *minimum* work for the maximum pay."

minute /mi nit/– a small amount of time, one 60th of an hour. Can also be a measurement unit of arc—that is, a *minute* of arc is one 60th of a degree of arc. Both *minutes* of time and *minutes* of arc can be further divided into 60 seconds.

Root
min means "small."

minute /mie nyut/– very small; of small importance; marked by close attention to details.

diminish – to make smaller or less important: "His wealth was *diminished* by his habit of spending too much."

minus – to take away, diminish by, deprive of; without: "*Minus* his mustache, I didn't recognize him." In math *minus* means "subtract."

diminutive – very small; a small replica of a larger object: "The boat was a *diminutive* of the *Queen Mary*." A *diminutive* is also a nickname that indicates smallness; for example, *Billy* is *diminutive* for *William,* and *kitchenette* is *diminutive* for *kitchen.*

minor – smaller: a *minor person* is someone who has not reached adulthood; a *minor theme* in music or a novel is less central than the major theme; a *minor course of study* is less time consuming than a major course of study. Don't spell it *miner,* because that's a person who works in a mine.

Activities

Name some *minutia* in your life.

A *minute* measures what two things?

Name some *diminutive* words.

What are some things that have *minors*?

Syllabification for correct spelling
_____
mi-nu-ti-a

A *perquisite* is a benefit or something extra or in addition to a regular salary. In slang it is called a *perk*. A *perk* might be an employer-paid health insurance policy or giving the employee a corner office. A tip given to the server after a meal is also a *perquisite*. A feudal lord might have inherited the *perquisite* of receiving a free baby lamb from each of his tenants every spring.

The prefix *per-* means "thoroughly" or "throughout," as in *perform*.

Root
quire or *queues* means "to gain" or "to seek."

question – an inquiry, doubt, or request. (*-tin* = noun form)

inquest – a judicial inquiry about facts related to an accident or death. (*in-* = in or toward)

requisition – a formal written order or request to fill a need. (*re-* = again or back)

acquire – to come into possession of something, often by unspecified means. (*ac-* = to)

conquer – to subdue by force or win by overcoming obstacles. (*con-* or *com-* = with)

Activities

The word *question* has three slightly different definitions. Give an example of each in a sentence.

When would you want an *inquest* if you had an accident?

What is the difference between *requisition* and *acquire*?

Syllabification for correct spelling

―――――――――
per-qui-site

How does *conquer* apply to both armies and mountain climbers?

Introspection means "self-examination" or looking within your own mind at your thoughts and feelings. After taking an action, you might wonder if it was right: Should you apologize or do you feel good about it? "Upon *introspection*, he asked himself, 'Why did I do that?'" (The prefix *intro-* means "in" or "within.")

Root

spect means "to see" or "to look."

inspect – to look at closely and perhaps critically in order to evaluate quality or errors. (*in-* = in or into)

circumspect – cautious or careful; literally, to look around before taking an action; to be discrete or watchful: "She was not very *circumspect* with her loud mouth when talking about other people." (*circum-* = around)

expectant – looking for something that is likely to happen. An audience can be *expectant* waiting for a rock star, and a mother can be *expectant* waiting for her child to be born. (*ex-* = out of)

prospect – a possible or probable outcome: "He had no *prospect* of getting rich." Also a possible buyer: "The Realtor brought over many *prospects* [prospective buyers] to view the house." (*pro-* = for or forward)

Activities

Would you *inspect* a car before you buy it?

_____ is often a synonym for pregnant.

Should you be *circumspect* when in a strange place?

Syllabification for correct spelling

_____

in-tro-spec-tion

What might the old *prospector* be hopeful for?

Desist means to stop or refrain from continuing an activity: "I want you to *desist* from this nonsense." Courts frequently issue a "cease and *desist*" order when they want to stop an action, such as loud noise in a neighborhood or excess unwanted attention from a frustrated lover. (*de-* = opposite)

Root
sist means "stand."

persist – to stubbornly go on or to continue to stand firm despite opposition. (*per-* = thoroughly)

resist – to stop or oppose some force; sort of the opposite of *persist*: "*Resist* the temptation to eat too much." (*re-* = again or back)

transistor – a tiny electronic device that is the basis of a computer's functioning. It either permits or does not permit an electronic current to pass through it. (*trans-* = across)

resistor – an electronic device that holds back electric current; a person who opposes an action: "War *resistors* won't join the army." (*re-* = back)

assist – to be helpful, to aid something or somebody. (*as-* = to)

exist – to have being: "Does happiness really *exist*?" "Deer *exist* in the forest." (*e-* = out)

coexist – to exist at the same time or in the same place as one or more other beings or things: "Trees and squirrels live happily together; they coexist." (*co-* = with)

Activities

Name two things that *coexist*.

From what would you like to *desist*?

If you quit in the middle, did you *persist*?

Do *assist* and *resist* mean the same thing?

Syllabification for correct spelling

_____

de-sist

A *dynasty* is a succession of rulers from the same family. Chinese history is usually organized by *dynasty*, a period in which one family supplied all the rulers. A *dynasty* can also be any power group that chooses its own successors, such as big businesses or other organizations.

Root
dyna means "power."

dynamite – a powerful explosive used for mining or destruction, made by mixing liquid nitroglycerin with an absorbent material to make it safer to handle; explosive. (*-ite* usually means a mineral.)

dynamic – very active or powerful: "He is a *dynamic* speaker."

dynamo – a generator, a device for converting mechanical power into electricity; also a person who is active and powerful: "She is a *dynamo*."

hydrodynamics – a branch of physics that deals with the power of water and other liquids; using the power of falling water to turn a turbine at a dam, or pressing on a car's brake pedal to put pressure on the brake fluid and stop the car. (*hydro-* = water)

dyne – a unit of force in the metric system: the amount of power needed to move one gram of weight one centimeter of distance in one second of time. In the American measurement system, the unit of force is called *horsepower*.

thermodynamics – the science of the relationship of heat and mechanical energy: "A steam engine works by *thermodynamics*."

Activities

How is *dynamite* used legally and illegally?

What word can mean either a machine or a person?

Is a knowledge of *hydrodynamics* useful?

How can you measure force?

Syllabification for correct spelling
_____
dy-nas-ty

Impressionism is a type of oil painting started by French artists in about the 1870s. It is less realistic or photographic than earlier styles of painting, but it still creates quite recognizable images by applying dabs or broad strokes of primarily unmixed color. Most art museums have some *impressionist* paintings, and some of the *impressionism* painters, such as Vincent van Gogh, are quite well known.

Impressionism is also a style of music.

Root
press means "press."

expressionism – a school of French painting that came after *impressionism* and fostered more abstract paintings. *Expressionism* is often confused with *impressionism* for good reason: the words sound alike and there is often not a clear and apparent distinction. Even art experts sometimes disagree on the matter.

oppress – to put down or crush. The prefix *op-* can mean "to," so *oppress* means "to press down": "The dictator *oppressed* the people."

repress – similar to *oppress* but meaning "to hold back": "He *repressed* all thoughts of violence." (*re-* = back)

express – to state directly and clearly: "She *expresses* herself well"; traveling at high speed: "The *express* train made few stops." (*ex-* = out)

Activities

Can you tell the difference between *impressionism* and *expressionism*?

What people in this world are *oppressed*?

Have you *repressed* any urges?

Syllabification for correct spelling
_____
im-pres-sion-ism

What characterizes *express* mail?

141 juxtapose /juks tuh poze   /juk' stə pōz'

Juxtapose means to place side-by-side or next to: "On the magazine page the picture was *juxtaposed* with the story." "The flowers were *juxtaposed* with the statue." The prefix *justa-* means "near" or "nearby."

impose – to apply as compulsory or as an obligation: "The new rule was *imposed* without any discussion." (*im-* = in)

Root
pos means to "set" or "put in place."

expose – to uncover or to open up: "The con man was *exposed* as a fraud." "Her *exposed* arm got sunburnt." (*ex-* = out)

interpose – to place between: "The reading of poems was *interposed* with music." "In the dance line, boys were *interposed* with girls."

repose – to rest or kick back: "He *reposed* on the couch after the race." (*re-* = back)

transpose – to change something into something else. For example, you can *transpose* English words into Latin words, and you can *transpose* the order of things, as in "the first shall be last." Typists sometimes accidentally *transpose* letters, causing errors, and in algebra you can *transpose* a term from one side of an equation to the other side. (*trans-* = across)

predispose – to make susceptible or more likely to happen: "He was *predisposed* to catch a cold because he was so tired." (*pre-* = before)

Activities

Name some things that are frequently *juxtaposed*.

Is paying income tax an *imposition*?

When are you in *repose*?

What causes you to be *predisposed* toward eating?

Syllabification for correct spelling
_____
jux-ta-pose

A *conservator* is a person appointed by a court to look after property for another person or organization: "When the youngster's parents were killed, a *conservator* was appointed to take care of the house and money." *Conservators* also repair and save old things such as paintings, historical buildings, and manuscripts. (*con-* = with)

Root
serv means "save."

conservative – one who wants to preserve tradition or the established order and sometimes opposes new ways. In politics, one who tends to oppose socialism or government control.

conservatory – a school specializing in the teaching of the arts or music, or sometimes a greenhouse for starting or growing plants.

observatory – a place for viewing the stars and planets through a telescope. (*ob-* = to)

reservoir – a storage place: "There is a large *reservoir* of water behind the dam." "The new president had a *reservoir* of goodwill." (*re-* = back)

reserve – to keep something in store for future use: "*Reserve* your strength, there is more work to do."

unreserved – not holding back, frank: "She is so *unreserved* that she will say anything." (*un-* = not)

conservation – saving something; frequently applied to ecology and saving the environment and natural resources. (*con-* = with)

Activities

Why are *conservators* necessary?

Do you know anyone who is a *conservative*?

What is taught in a *conservatory*?

What is your community doing about *conservation*?

Syllabification for correct spelling

—————————————

con-ser-va-tor

143 suffice /suh fice /sə fĭs'/

Suffice means to have enough or an amount sufficient to satisfy or fulfill needs: "I hope the third pancake will *suffice* to relieve your hunger." "In case of trouble, two police officers should *suffice*."

office – both a place to work and a position: "His *office* is in that building." "She holds the *office* of vice president; therefore she is an *officer* of the corporation." (*of-* = work)

edifice – a large building such as a church or government building.

Root
fic means "to do" or "to make."

sacrifice – giving up something or making an offering to God: "He *sacrificed* going to the party so he could study." "The ancient Jews *sacrificed* (killed) animals as an offering to God." (*sacr-* = sacred)

deficit – lacking in some quality or amount and thus not being complete: "The mistake was caused by a *deficit* of common sense." "A *deficit* of income caused the debt to increase." (*de-* = from)

benefit – something that is good or positive for well being: "The new job had more *benefits*, including paid health insurance and a retirement plan."

artificial – man-made, not made by nature. (*art-* = skill)

Activities

What *suffices* to meet your need for recreation?

Name an *edifice* in your community.

Are *benefit* and *deficit* opposites?

Name three things that are *artificial* and three things that are natural.

Syllabification for correct spelling
_____
suf-fice

A *confectioner* is a candymaker or a cake decorator. So cakes, candies, and sometimes ice cream are *confections*. In fact, a *confection* could be anything edible that has sugar in it, as well as preserved fruits, nuts, and roots.

 Confection can also function as a metaphor meaning "fancy," "sweet," or "delicious"; it can be applied to music, art, or architecture; and used in either a positive or negative manner. (*con-* = with)

Root
fec means "to make" or "to do."

affection – a kind feeling, warm attachment, or fondness. *Affection* is used often because it is less strong than *love*. (*af-* = to)

affectation – Watch out: *affectation* is not closely related to *affection*. An *affectation* (note the extra syllable) means putting on a false manner or way of speaking, such as a temporary British accent, with the hope of impressing someone.

disaffection – withdrawal of liking or warm feeling; the opposite of affection. (*dis-* = opposite)

perfect – without fault or error. (*per-* = thoroughly)

affect /ay fekt/ – used in psychology for any emotion; mental rather than physical change.

effect – Watch out again: *effect* sounds like *affect*, but it means "result" or "outcome": "What is the *effect* of driving while drunk?" (*ef-* = out)

Activities

Name some specific kinds of *confections*.

For what do you have *affection*?

For what do you have *disaffection*?

Fill in the blank with either *affect* or *effect*:
 "Do you like the _____ of the new rules?"

Syllabification for correct spelling
_____
con-fec-tion-er

A *malcontent* is one unhappy person—someone who perhaps carries a grudge based on some real or imagined grievance: "He became a *malcontent* when he was not promoted." A *malcontent* could also be unhappy with the government and seek to change it. In the extreme, he could be called a rebel.

This word has two prefixes: *mal-* meaning "bad" and *con-* meaning "with."

Root
tent or *ten* means "to hold."

con tent' – satisfied with what you have; not complaining.

con' tent – Note the shift in accent from the second to the first syllable, which changes the meaning completely. Here *content* means what is inside of something: "The *content* of the letter was that he was fired." "What are the *contents* of that suitcase?" (The two *contents* are heterophones.)

contention /con ten shun/ – Here is another big shift in meaning for a seemingly closely related word. A *contention* is a disagreement, perhaps an argument, either polite or violent.

countenance /cown tah nence/ – a facial expression indicating mood: "Her *countenance* indicated utter calm."

detention – holding in custody, keeping after school.

tenant – a renter; one who holds property.

tenet – a principle or belief held to be true: "The right to a fair trial is a *tenet*."

Activities

Do you know any *malcontents*?

What *contentions* are reported on in today's newspaper?

What are the two ways that *content* is pronounced?

What is a *tenet*?

Syllabification for correct spelling
_____
mal-con-tent

In a range of numbers that are ranked in order of size, the *median* is the middle number; half of the numbers are above and half are below. This is sometimes called the *average*, but it is not the same as the arithmetical *mean* or the average obtained by adding up all the numbers and dividing the total by the quantity of numbers.

The *median* is useful when you have one or two very large numbers and a lot of smaller numbers. For example, the average price of a house in your area is frequently a *median* because although most of the houses will sell for around one price, there may be a mansion on the corner that will throw off the arithmetical average (*mean*) when you ask, "What is the average price of a house in that area?" A *median* can also be a separating place, such as the *median* strip of land between two lanes of traffic.

Root
medi means "middle."

mediator – someone who helps two opposing parties find a settlement and meet somewhere in the middle of their different demands. (*or-* = person)

mediation – the process of finding an agreement between two different demands; often used in labor negotiations in which the union wants higher wages and management wants lower wages.

mediocre – middle quality, maybe moderate, but not high quality.

immediate – without intervening time; without intervention of space or substance: "He placed the second block *immediately* after the first block." (*im-* = not)

Activities

Collect a group of numbers, such as the height of everyone in a class, and calculate the *median* and the arithmetical average (*mean*).

Name several contexts in which a *mediator* could be used.

What are some things that are *mediocre*?

What are some words that are antonyms (meaning the opposite) for *immediate*?

Syllabification for correct spelling

———————————
me-di-an

Gestate means to carry in the uterus. For humans, *gestation* takes nine months after becoming pregnant. It can also apply to ideas: "It took a long time to *gestate* the outline for a new play."

gesture – to use the body, particularly the hands and arms, to express ideas and emotions: "I knew by his wild *gestures* that he was excited."

gesticulate – to use many gestures: "He *gesticulated* continuously throughout his speech."

Root
gest means "carry."

digest – to move food through the stomach so it can be broken down and absorbed; the internal process of changing food for use by the body; chemical and biological reactions to change in a mixture; the summarizing or understanding of an idea or thought: "It took a while to *digest* the letter saying that she was fired." (*di-* = apart)

ingest – to eat; to put food or pills into the stomach: "Don't *ingest* fruit until you wash it." (*in-* = in)

suggest – to bring up an idea for consideration. (*sug-* = under)

congestion – overcrowding: "The *congestion* on the freeway was bad." (*con-* = together)

Activities

Do dogs *gestate*?

Use a *gesture* to show that you are glad, mad, or sad.

Explain the difference between *digest* and *ingest*.

Where have you seen *congestion*?

Syllabification for correct spelling

_____

ges-tate

Distend means to expand in all directions, to stretch out or enlarge: "An infected finger can *distend* so that the swelling becomes obvious." "*Distended* profits might be nice in the short run but should not be relied on for the long run." (*dis-* = apart)

extend – to stretch out: "*Extend* your arm toward me." "The bank *extends* credit to local businesses." (*ex-* = out)

Root
tend means "stretch."

contend – to strive with determination against an opposing team or to solve a problem: "The principal *contends* daily with absenteeism." "I have to *contend* with an aggressive little brother." (*con-* = with)

attend – to pay attention to; to "*attend* to business"; to be present; to *attend* school. (*at-* = to)

intend – to mean: "What did you *intend* by that remark?" "He *intended* his comments to be funny." "She *intends* to pay the bill." (*in-* = in)

portend – to be an omen or forewarning: "Dark clouds *portend* rain."

pretend – to appear (perhaps falsely) to be something: "She *pretended* to be sad but really she wasn't." (*pre-* = before)

Activities

Name several things that can be *extended*.

With what must a police officer *contend*?

What do poor grades *portend*?

When do you *pretend*?

Syllabification for correct spelling

──────────
dis-tend

Encompass means to form a circle around something, to *encircle*: "The tall trees *encompass* the meadow." It can also mean *envelop*, as in "The boat was *encompassed* by a thick fog." (*en-* = in; *com-* = with)

pass – to go around or proceed, as in "*pass* that slow car"; a place for passage, such as a mountain *pass* that you go through; a ticket for free admission.

Root
pass means "step" or "go."

compassion – sympathy for someone in trouble; being in step with another person's feelings: "I have *compassion* for my friend with a broken leg." (*com-* = with)

surpass – to go beyond someone or something: "Because he studied hard, his grades *surpassed* those of his classmates." (*sur-* = over or beyond)

trespass – to unlawfully invade property or someone's rights: "The 'no *trespassing*' sign means 'keep out.'"

compass – a device for showing magnetic North, used in determining direction; a device used in drawing circles: "When lost in the forest, a *compass* is a handy tool."

passion – very strong feeling for something or someone: "He has a *passion* for football."

Activities

Name some other things that can be *encompassed*.

When does someone need *compassion*?

What is an area in your life in which you *surpass* others?

Give two meanings for the word *compass*.

Syllabification for correct spelling

_____

en-com-pass

Actuate means to cause an action or put something in motion: "The cut in pay could *actuate* many employees to resign." "The FBI agent was aware that any motion could *actuate* the explosion of the bomb."

actor – a person who does performances on stage, for television, or in movies: "The *actor* who played the villain in the play was so believable that when she was killed the audience cheered."

Root
act means "to do."

transact – to do or carry to completion business negotiations or other activities: "The company would not *transact* business on Sunday."

radioactivity – the property or characteristic of certain elements (such as uranium or carbon-14) that spontaneously produces energetic particles and emits radiation: "The *radioactivity* in kryptonite was the one thing that could kill Superman."

actual – done, real, or factual; existing at the present time or currently: "He thought he would have no money left but his *actual* expenses were less than what he thought they would be." "The ship's *actual* position is twenty-two miles due east and not west of Catalina."

exactitude – the quality of being precise, correct, or an exact likeness: "The *exactitude* of his directions was such that a child could have found the house."

Activities

Tell about a time when selfishness *actuated* you to do something.

List three kinds of *transactions*.

How does the word *actor* demonstrate the root *act,* "to do"?

Under what circumstances is it important to utilize *exactitude*?

Syllabification for correct spelling

ac-tu-ate

151 attribute /at trib yoot /əˈ trə byōot'

An *attribute* /at' tri bute/ is a characteristic of someone or something: "Kindness is an attribute that many people look for in a friend."
   Attribute /a trib' bute/ (note the shift in pronunciation) means "to explain something": "He *attributed* the loss of the baseball game to the poor weather conditions." (*at-* = to)

tribune – a Roman army officer or public official who gives protection to the people.

Root
tribe means "to give."

distribute – to divide and give out in shares: "The teacher usually calls on a student to *distribute* the supplies for the day's activity." (*dis-* = opposite of)

contribution – the act of giving (money, time, knowledge, assistance) to a person or organization that has a charitable purpose: "The accumulated *contributions* to the school allowed for a brand-new theater to be built." (*con-* = together)

tribe – any group of people united by ties of ancestry, community, customs, and traditions and who have the same leader: "Many Native American *tribes* live in the same area."

retribution – the giving of a reward or punishment for a previous action: "The *retribution* for his crimes was five years in prison." "In *retribution* for his heroic act he received a key to the city."

Activities

List three positive *attributes* of your own or of one of your friends.

What organizations in your community do you think need *contributions*?

How is a democratic government different from a *tribe*?

Are prisons based on *retribution*?

Syllabification for correct spelling

at-trib-ute

152 emissary /eh miss sair ee   /em' ə ser' ē

An *emissary* is someone chosen (typically an agent) to go on a mission or an errand of importance: "The president sent an *emissary* to negotiate for peace." "The gang thought he was a friend but he turned out to be an *emissary* for the police."

permissive – given permission or allowed freedom: "The library's *permissive* environment allowed for us to do research on the computers, use the reference books, and make photocopies"; always being accepting or tolerant: "The teacher's *permissive* behavior made the students think they could get away with anything." (*per-* = through)

Root
miss means "to send."

omission – leaving out: "The *omission* of her name from the list meant that she was not nominated to be class president."

transmissible – capable of being passed on or spread out: "The grandmother's *transmissible* assets to the family were listed in her will." (*trans-* = beyond)

submissive – ready to yield to the will of others: "The *submissive* servants would pick up after the rude children."

promissory – giving a promise or assurance: "The *promissory* terms of the sale stated that he could return the items a full year after purchase if something went wrong." (*pro-* = beyond)

Activities

How is being an *emissary* different from being a messenger?

What are some *promissory* terms in the Bill of Rights?

Explain how *permissive* can be both a positive and a negative trait.

What is a situation in your life from which you do not want to be *omitted*?

Syllabification for correct spelling

---

em-is-sar-y

153 oligarchy /ol uh gar kee /ol' i gär' kē

Oligarchy means rule by a few or a small group. The group can rule a country, a business, or any other organization: "We must get rid of that *oligarchy* so that the people's voice can be heard." *Oligarchy* does not usually apply to an elected or openly appointed board of directors or similar body; it might be a secret group of persons seeking personal gain. (*olig-* = few)

It can refer to a person, such as a chief, or it can mean a quality or characteristic.

Root
archy means "rule."

archbishop – the ruler of other bishops.

archangel – the ruler of other angels.

archduke – the ruler of other dukes.

archfool – the ruler of other fools.

archcapitalist – the ruler of other capitalists.

archenemy – the ruler of other enemies.

anarchist – someone opposed to any kind of rule; someone who wants little or no government. (*an-* = without)

archives – the main place where governmental or other organizational records, particularly historical records, are kept.

patriarch – ruler of a family, clan, or religious organization; an elder and respected religious or organization leader. (*patri-* = father)

Activities

Would an *anarchist* like an *archbishop*?

Might an *archduke* have *archives*?

Could a young person be a *patriarch*?

Ten people who run a country could be called an _____.

Syllabification for correct spelling
_____
ol-i-gar-chy

154 covert /ko vert /kō' vərt

Covert means secret or hidden. A covert operator is a spy. A covert agreement is a secret agreement. A covert cave is hidden and usually in a place unknown by others.

cover – a blanket or an upper coat of paint; to guard or protect: "*Cover* me with this gun while I go ahead"; to hide or conceal: "He tried to *cover* up the crime."

undercover – to act in secret: "Spies work *undercover* to accomplish their goals."

discover – to remove a cover or find something previously unknown: "He *discovered* in the doctor's office that he had a broken bone." (*dis-* = not or opposite)

recover – to get back. You can *recover* your health from an illness and you can *recover* from many other problems such as business failure or friendship loss. (*re-* = back)

coverlet – a small blanket, bedspread, or other type of covering. (*-let* = small)

irrevocable – unable to be gotten back; incapable of being recalled: "Money paid for some tickets is *irrevocable*, even if you do not use them." (*ir-* = not)

> **Root**
> *cover* means "cover," and is both a root and a word.

Activities

Do you know of any *covert* places?

Could a *discoverer* go *undercover*?

What kinds of tickets are *irrevocable*?

Can a baby's crib use a *coverlet*?

> **Syllabification for correct spelling**
> _____
> **co-vert**

Incipient means "beginning" or "about to become apparent": "The *incipient* stage of the disease may not come out for a few days." "*Incipient* causes of a war occur at the very beginning, before the shooting starts."

anticipate – the root of this word means "before being seized," but it usually means to think in advance of some action or situation that may or might happen: "He *anticipated* trouble when he saw that girl."

Root
cip means to "take" or "seize."

principle – a fundamental truth, law, or belief: "Telling the truth is always the best *principle*." (*prin-* = first)

principal – the first person, one who is in charge or responsible: "The school *principal* is responsible for seeing that *principles* are maintained." It can also mean a main or first cause, such as, "What is the *principal* cause of global warming?" (*principle* and *principal* are homophones) (*prin-* = first)

municipal – of local government, usually of a city: "Local police are *municipal* employees." (*muni-* = function)

participate – to take part in something, to be actively engaged: "Did you *participate* in the play?" (*part-* = part)

recipe – instructions for cooking; a medicine compound (prescription); or some other procedure. (*re-* = back or again)

Activities

What are some *incipient* steps in starting a business?

Name several things that you *anticipate*.

Give some examples of uses for *principle* and *principal*.

How are *recipe* and *participate* related in meaning?

Syllabification for correct spelling

_____

in-cip-i-ent

Concentric means that two or more things have a common center or a common axis. A small circle and a larger circle around it are *concentric* if they have a common center. A slice of a cone near the top and a parallel slice of the same cone near the bottom are *concentric*. (*con-* = with)

centrifugal – moving away from the center. A washing machine, for example, spins the clothes at the end of the cycle to extract most of the water and it is the *centrifugal* force of the spinning that causes the water to move out. *Centrifugal* force is a little like gravity: hold a rock on a string still and gravity will pull the string down toward the ground, but spin the rock above your head and the string will move out parallel to the ground and away from your hand, which is the center of the spinning action. (*-fug* = flee)

Root
centr means "center."

eccentric /ek sen trik/ – odd or unconventional: "The old lady was truly *eccentric*; she always wore a tuxedo." (*ec-* = from)

decentralize – to move away from the center; scatter: "The houses were *decentralized* and spread out over the countryside." "The power of the government was so *decentralized* that the new leader couldn't figure out how to change things." (*de-* = from; *-ize* = verb form)

concentrate – to bring toward the center, to focus: "In order to study you must *concentrate* on the subject." "The can of orange juice is *concentrated*; most of the water has been removed."

Activities

Draw some *concentric* circles.

Do some demonstrations of *centrifugal* force using a salad spinner or a weight on a string.

Name a person who is a bit *eccentric*.

Does the U.S. Constitution demand *decentralized* power?

Syllabification for correct spelling

con-cen-tric

A *miscreant* is a thoroughly bad guy. He engages in vice and things evil. He is a villain, a wretch who is vile and detestable. Besides all that, historically he is a heretic and doesn't even believe in the same religion you do. (*mis-* = bad)

credentials – formal qualifications that give credit or confidence. A *credential* can be a diploma, a letter, or a document that says the person has demonstrated achievement or is entitled to fulfill certain duties: "Teachers and doctors have *credentials* issued by the state." (*-ial* = related to)

Root
cre or *cred* means "to trust" or "to believe."

incredulous – not believable, beyond belief: "His tall stories are simply *incredulous*." (*in-* = not)

incredible – same meaning as *incredulous*.

discredit – not to believe, to destroy confidence, to lose respect: "The findings of the report were *discredited*." "The *discredited* leader was voted out of office." (*di-* = not)

credible – believable; opposite of *incredulous*.

creed – a statement of beliefs or principles, especially religious beliefs.

accredit – to recognize as reputable or officially approved: "I hope you go to an *accredited* college." "She *accredits* her vitamin pills with enabling her success in athletics."

Activities

What are some things a *miscreant* might do?

Do your teachers have *credentials*?

What is the difference between *incredulous* and *incredible*?

To what do you *accredit* your success?

Syllabification for correct spelling

———————————
mis-cre-ant

A *courtesy* can be a gift: "The birthday cake was provided *courtesy* of the ABC Company." Or it can be well-mannered behavior: "She performed with *courtesy* at the funeral."

court – a group of high-ranking persons such as dukes and princes who attended parties and official functions of the king. The *court* had rules of social behavior and manners. A *court* is also a judge and sometimes a jury assembled to administer justice and uphold the law or settle disputes.

Root
court refers to a royal court

courtier – a member of the king's court: "The prince was the most handsome *courtier*."

courting – seeking favor from someone: "He was *courting* the pretty girl hoping to seek her hand in marriage."

courtship – a period of courting: "Their *courtship* lasted for a year."

courteous – having a polished manner, often to show respect; behavior suitable for a court: "He was very *courteous* to her father."

discourteous – rude, not acting in a courtly manner: "She was so *discourteous* that she did not even introduce her friend to her parents." (*dis-* = opposite, not)

curtsy – a gesture used by women to show respect by lowering the body slightly with bending of the knees.

Activities

If you receive a book with a note saying it is *courtesy* of the publisher, do you have to pay for it?

Do civil *courts* have *courtiers*?

Demonstrate a *curtsy*.

Contrast some *courteous* and *discourteous* behavior.

Syllabification for correct spelling

———————

cour-te-sy

A *demagogue* is a bad leader, sometimes called a "rabble rouser," who makes extravagant claims or promises, perhaps for his own personal gain. Historically, a *demagogue* did not have such a bad association; the *demagogue* was a speaker or leader who was a champion of the common people.

Root
demo or *dema* means "people."

democracy – rule by the people. (*-cracy* = rule)

democrat – one who believes in rule by the people; *Democrat* capitalized means a particular political party in the United States. (*-crat* = rule or an advocate of a theory of government or a member of a dominant class, for example, an aristocrat; both have to do with ruling)

demographer – a person who studies the growth, migration, and other vital statistics of human populations.

epidemic – a communicable disease affecting many people, causing widespread illness; a scourge on the people: "In the Middle Ages, the plague was an *epidemic*."*Epidemic* can also mean large and widespread trouble for people, such as an "*epidemic* of grasshoppers." (*epi-* = on)

endemic – belonging to a particular region or people: "Starvation is *endemic* in certain areas of Africa." "Some weeds are *endemic* to coastal regions." (*en-* = on)

pandemic – similar to *epidemic* but more serious because it implies a very wide area: "AIDS is *pandemic*; it is spreading to the whole world." (*pan-* = all)

Activities

Would you vote for a *demagogue*?

Could a *Democrat* live in a republic?

Which would be worse for the world: a *pandemic* or an *epidemic*?

Could an animal be *endemic*?

Syllabification for correct spelling
———————————
dem-a-gogue

In mathematics, a *dividend* is a number being divided. For example, in 6 ÷ 2 = 3, 6 is the *dividend*. In stock companies, the *dividend* is the amount of money each share gets when the profit being distributed is divided by the number of shares.

divide – to separate into pieces or groups. You can *divide* a number, a country, an idea, and a lot of other things.

divisible – can be divided. (*-able* = capable of)

divisive – tending to create divisions or disunity: "She was very *divisive* and caused our group to separate into small factions." (*-ive* = inclined to)

individual – a single or separate thing; often used to mean a single human being, but can also mean an animal or one of many other things.

individualism – the tendency to do one's own thing without much concern for others' opinions: "A little *individualism* is good, but too much is bad." (*-ism* = state or quality of)

devise – to invent or plan something new or unique: "She *devised* a new type of engine."

device – something new or useful: "She installed a *device* for saving gas." "The accountant knew a law that was a *device* for lowering taxes."

Root
divi means "to separate into pieces or groups."

Activities

If you own stock, the money you are paid yearly if the company shares a profit is called a _____.

What can someone do to be *divisive*?

Give some examples of *individualism*.

Is a *devise* a thing?

Syllabification for correct spelling
_____
div-i-dend

Vivisection means the action of cutting into or dissecting a living body in order to understand better how the body works: "The *vivisection* of his heart would not only save the patient's life, it would also give the surgeons information on how to prevent heart disease."

sectarian – something or someone who embraces a particular religious faith and is limited to believing all or part of it.

Root
sect **means "to cut."**

sector – a distinct part of something (society, a town, the economy): "The education *sector* of the government is relying on the lottery to fund its new projects." "Each police officer patrols his or her own *sector*."

dissect – to separate into pieces and expose the parts of (such as an animal) for scientific examination: "In science class the students *dissected* the heart of a sheep and studied its parts." (*di-* = double)

intersect – to section off by meeting at a cross point: "In class today we practiced making *intersecting* lines to create right angles." (*in-* = within)

insect – a small invertebrate animal whose body is segmented so one can easily see the different parts: "The campers turned over the *insect* and studied the six segments of its underbelly." (*in-* = within)

sect – a group of people that breaks away from the common religion and adheres to a particular religious faith.

Activities

How is a *vivisection* beneficial to scientists?

List some *insects* that you would find in your home.

What *sector* of your town has a lot of stores?

List some things that can *intersect*.

Syllabification for correct spelling
_____
viv-i-sec-tion

Coherence means different parts sticking together to become unified: "The *coherence* within the political party was the reason for the candidate's success." It also means having clarity or intelligence: "The plan lacked *coherence* and the players were running lost in all different directions." (*co-* = together)

adhere – to cling and stay attached: "The mud adhered to her shoes as she ran through the field." (*ad-* = to)

Root
here means "the act," "the attachment," or "to stick."

inherent – strongly rooted and essential; generally applied to a personal characteristic or understanding: "The child had an *inherent* understanding that he should stay away from strangers." (*in-* = within)

heresy – a religious opinion that is different from church or community belief and considered dangerous: "The rise of *heresy* within the church was strong enough to start a war."

heritage – something that stays within a group of people and is passed on to other generations: "The way we are treating the Earth will leave our children with a *heritage* of pollution."

heredity – the passing on of genetic (gene-based) characteristics from parents to their offspring.

Activities

Do you have a *heritage*?

How has *heresy* been viewed differently throughout history?

When you were young, what were things you knew *inherently*?

Syllabification for correct spelling
_____
co-her-ence

List three things that help things *adhere* to surfaces.

Notoriety is the characteristic of being widely recognized for doing or creating something (making your mark on society): "Some actors get into show business not because they love acting but for the *notoriety* that comes with being in the spotlight." "As the school continued its community service program it gained *notoriety*." "Even criminals can get *notoriety*."

Root
note means "to mark."

notion – a person's impression of something known, experienced, or imagined: "Her *notion* of the United States was that it was a land where anything was possible." *Notion* can also mean an uncertain or general understanding of something: "His *notion* that the teacher was scary wasn't based on any facts."

notorious – publicly noted as having a particular trait: "He was *notorious* for throwing the biggest and best parties."

notice – an announcement giving information or warning: "The farmer posted a 'keep out' *notice*."

connote – to suggest and have significance by association: "Poverty *connotes* misery."

notarize – to certify or acknowledge: "The marriage certificate wasn't valid until it was *notarized* by a judge."

annotation – a note added for explanation: "Footnotes are *annotations* to the text."

Activities

What are some things people do to establish *notoriety*?

In what kinds of books would you see *annotations*?

List two types of *notices* that give information and two types that give warning.

What are some *notions* that people can have about going to college?

Syllabification for correct spelling

─────────────

no-to-ri-e-ty

Immune means to be protected from something or someone. When talking about illness it means having developed antibodies to protect one's body from a particular disease: "The little girl had chicken pox and could be around only people who were *immune* to this disease." *Immune* also means not responsive to something or someone: "The judge was *immune* to the murderer's pleas for mercy."

Root
mune means
"gift."

communal – something owned by everyone in a group: "Everyone who shopped at the store appreciated the *communal* jar of pennies at the counter." (*com-* = before)

remunerate – to pay back or reward fairly: "To *remunerate* the neighbors for watching our dog, I have promised to feed their cat while they are on vacation." (*re-* = again)

communication – the giving and receiving of thoughts, opinions, and information by speaking, writing, and signs: "If the world's leaders were all in *communication*, would there still be war?" (*com-* = before)

munificent – free in giving: "The orphanage greatly appreciated his *munificent* gift of a hundred thousand dollars."

excommunicate – to expel a person or persons from membership or from receiving the gifts and privileges of the church. (*ex-* = not)

Activities

Have you ever been in a *communal* swimming pool?

Describe an incident in your life in which there was a misunderstanding due to poor *communication*.

If you work for a company would you expect *remuneration*?

What is the most *munificent* gift you have ever given or received?

Syllabification for correct spelling

———————

im-mune

Resuscitate means to revive or restore from a state of seeming death: "The drowning victim lay deadly still, but after many CPR attempts the paramedics were able to *resuscitate* her." "Some very ill old people state clearly that they do not want to be *resuscitated* (DNR, do not *resuscitate*) in the event that they go into a coma, which means they would not want to be hooked up to any machines that will operate their organs for them." (*re-* = again)

Root
cite means
"to call."

citation – an official call to appear before a court; a reference to another source when writing a formal paper.

excitement – the state of being emotionally aroused or worked up: "The music caused such *excitement* that the students and teachers all began to dance." (*ex-* = out of)

incite – to urge a person or a group of people into immediate action: "The death of the boy *incited* the crowd to enter into a huge riot." (*in-* = toward)

citadel – a fortress in a city that is used to defend and control the people of the city: "The *citadel* stood strong throughout the barbarian invasion."

citizen – a native or adopted person who is now part of a government. Usually a *citizen* can vote and has other rights and responsibilities.

Activities

When a conversation dies, what are some ways to *resuscitate* it?

Describe a moment when you were filled with *excitement*.

If you could be a *citizen* of a country other than your native country, which country would you choose?

List some famous leaders who could *incite* groups of people to action.

Syllabification for correct spelling

_____

re-sus-ci-tate

Fortify means to make strong and secure, especially in the face of attack: "The townspeople had to *fortify* their homes for the coming hurricane." "The students were encouraged to *fortify* their opinions with facts." "The soldiers built dugouts and put up barricades to *fortify* the area in case of an attack."

Root
fort means "strong."

fortitude – a mental and emotional strength that gives a person courage in the face of difficulty, danger, or temptation: "The firefighters' *fortitude* did not waver in the face of the enormous burning building." (*-tude* = state or quality of)

forte /for tay/ – a person's strong point, that at which he or she excels: "Because his *forte* was music, he had the ability to play a song after hearing it only once."

fortress – a large secure place, often established to set up defense for a town. (*-ess* = noun suffix)

effort – the use of physical or mental strength to accomplish something: "It took great *effort* for her to finish medical school." (*ef-* = out)

fortify – to add material in order to strengthen or enrich something: "The *fortification* of the tree house included an old mattress, plywood, and kids armed with water balloons." (*-ify* = verb suffix; *-tion* = noun suffix)

Activities

List one way you can *fortify* an area, a sports team, or an idea.

What *efforts* do you make to be successful at school?

How might someone develop a *forte*?

List some situations that require committed *fortitude*.

Syllabification for correct spelling
_____
for-ti-fy

Construct means to build by combining or arranging parts to make a whole: "The teacher took the phrases and descriptive words to *construct* a compound sentence." "To *construct* the garden the children gathered scrap wood, seeds, rocks, and soil." (*con-* = together)

instruct – to build with knowledge and provide information and guidance. (*in-* = within)

Root
stru means to "build."

structure – something built of parts into a whole: "The *structure* stood so tall you could see it from miles away."

construe – to build understanding based on a set of circumstances: "She was screaming so loudly that I *construed* her actions to be hostile." (*con-* = together)

instrument – an object used to build something or get something done: "The hammer was the *instrument* used to build the platform." "A compass is an *instrument* used in navigation." (*in-* = within)

obstruct – to build or pile up in a way that hinders: "The gravel pile *obstructed* the vision of the tourists." (*ob-* = on or around)

Activities

What things in your house could you pull together to *construct* a fort?

How would you *instruct* someone to make a peanut butter and jelly sandwich?

What meaning could you *construe* if you walked into the classroom and everyone was under their desk?

List three *instruments* and what they can be used for.

Syllabification for correct spelling

con-struct

Sensation is an awareness of feeling (such as of heat or pain) due to stimulation of one or more of the senses (taste, sight, hearing, smell, touch): "As he ran away he felt in his head the stinging *sensation* caused by the other boy's punches." *Sensation* can also mean "exceptional" or "outstanding": "The crowd cheered for Jones, the new slam-dunk *sensation*."

Root
sens means "feel."

sensory – perceiving through the five basic senses (touch, sight, sound, smell, and taste): "The child was a *sensory* learner and better able to learn the alphabet by writing it in shaving cream."

sensor – an instrument or machine that perceives and measures the levels of such things as light, temperature, or radiation: "A smoke detector is a *sensor*."

sensitive – easily hurt or damaged: "The boy had just lost his dog and was *sensitive* about the idea of getting a new pet." *Sensitive* can also mean being "aware of the attitudes and feelings of others": "She was *sensitive* to the new student, and went and sat with him when no one else would."

insensate – without human feeling; cold, cruel, or brutal: "The *insensate* ruler didn't notice the starving people among his population."

senses – the abilities of sight, hearing, smell, taste, and touch, by which humans and animals recognize stimuli from outside or inside the body.

Activities

What kind of *sensations* can occur when you are on stage in front of hundreds of people?

How does being *insensate* affect those around you?

What are the five *senses*?

List three things to which you are *sensitive*.

Syllabification for correct spelling

―――――――――

sen-sa-tion

Infuse means to penetrate someone or something with something else that changes the person or thing, usually for the better: "The coach could *infuse* any team with pride." "The new project *infused* the office with a sense of purpose." "Christmas morning *infused* the children with excitement." (*in-* = within)

Root
fus means
"to pour."

fusion – the process of liquefying and combining elements by heat: "At the right temperature, the *fusion* of the solid metals could occur." *Fusion* can also mean to become united or blended: "The solo singer was nice, but the *fusion* of all the singers together was very powerful." (*-ion* = noun suffix)

effuse – to pour out, especially emotion: "Her home *effuses* warmth and hospitality." (*ef-* = out)

transfusion – to transfer blood or other fluid into a vein or artery of a person or animal. (*trans-* = through)

diffuse – to spread or scatter widely or thinly: "The lemonade was too strong, so we *diffused* it with water." (*di-* = two)

suffuse – to pour beneath or spread through or over with liquid, color, or light: "The sunset on the desert's horizon tonight is *suffused* with red, gold, and pink." (*suf-* = under)

Activities

What would you *infuse* a cake with to make it tastier?

How is *fusion* used in science?

List three areas that could be *suffused* with light or color.

What kinds of characteristics do you *effuse*?

Syllabification for correct spelling

_____

in-fuse

Loquacious means being an excessive talker: "The *loquacious* girls were the cause of the high phone bill." "Sometimes a *loquacious* manner can be annoying." "The *loquacious* teacher took forever to get to the point and made many digressions."

soliloquy – a speech addressed to oneself: "One of Shakespeare's most famous *soliloquies* is that of Hamlet talking to himself about whether or not he should live or die." (*soli-* = alone)

Root
loq means "speak."

colloquial – of or relating to familiar or informal conversation: "On the football field the boys speak in *colloquial* English." (*col-* = with)

ventriloquist – a performer who projects her voice into a wooden dummy and carries on an apparent conversation with it: "The *ventriloquist* made the puppet talk in different voices." (*ventr* = abdomen)

eloquence – the use of language with fluency and ability: "The *eloquence* of his speech was proof that he had been well educated." (*e-* = out)

obloquy – abusive language aimed at a person or thing, used mostly by a group of people calling someone bad names. (*ob-* = against)

Activities

What famous people would you consider *loquacious* and why?

In a play, what does a *soliloquy* help you to understand?

What are the benefits to having *eloquence*?

Have you ever heard any *obloquy*?

Syllabification for correct spelling
_____
lo-qua-cious

Cognizant means to have knowledge or mental awareness: "He was *cognizant* of the trouble brewing in that country." "She was *cognizant* that someone was looking at her." (*co-* = with)

ignorant – lacking knowledge, awareness, or understanding; generally stupid: "He was *ignorant* of the coming rainstorm." (*i-* = not)

Root
gni or *gno* means "to know."

diagnosis – identification of a disease or of the cause of other problems: "The doctor *diagnosed* the patient's fever as flu." "The mechanic *diagnosed* the engine problem." (*dia-* = through; *-sis* = process)

recognize – to become aware, to come to know about something. (*re-* = back)

prognosis – a prediction about the probable course of a disease or other action. (*pro-* = before)

agnostic – one who maintains doubt about the existence of God. (*a-* = not)

gnostic /nahs tik/ – one who has knowledge of God or spiritual mysteries; a follower of Gnosticism, an early Christian religious group.

gnome /nohm/ – a mythical creature who knows about hidden treasure; a forest elf.

know – to have information about or experience of something.

Activities

What are you *cognizant* of right now?

Name areas in which you are *ignorant*.

What is the *prognosis* if you get AIDS?

What does an *agnostic* doubt?

Syllabification for correct spelling
—————————
cog-ni-zant

Reduplication means doubling something. In fact, it actually means about the same thing as *duplication* or *replica*: "Stop all this *reduplication* of effort, it is costing too much time." *Reduplication* also applies to a special kind of word that doubles two similar sounds, such as *geegaw, hanky-panky, pell-mell, bonbon,* or *claptrap.*

Root
du means "two."

duplicate – copy of an original; to produce another copy of something: "Fill out this form in *duplicate*." "Don't *duplicate* another person's original art." (*pli* = fold or layer)

duel – a fight between two persons.

dual – having two things, two parts, or two ideas: "His car has *dual* tailpipes." "The poem has dual themes, one hidden and one obvious." (*duel* and *dual* are homophones)

dubious – doubtful, skeptical, unclear: "Her claim to be related to the queen was *dubious*."

deuce – a card with the number 2 or two dots on it; the side of a die (half of a pair of dice) with two dots.

indubitable – not having two meanings, unquestionable, beyond doubt: "Her refusal was *indubitable*."

duplicitous – being deceptive by preaching one thing and acting out another; untrustworthy, showing bad faith, doing double dealing: "Because he had been *duplicitous*, the deal crashed." (*pli* = fold or layer)

Activities

Can you think of another *reduplication* word?

What letters cause confusion between *duel* and *dual*?

How are *dubious* and *duplicitous* similar and how are they different?

Are two aces a *deuce*?

Syllabification for correct spelling

---

re-du-pli-ca-tion

Perfidy is the quality of being dishonest or disloyal, and the act of betrayal. You don't want this kind of person for a friend, a business partner, or a political leader: "The *perfidy* of a few politicians gives a bad name to all politicians." "Because of the Duke's *perfidy* in giving information to the enemy, the King had him beheaded."

fidelity – faithfulness, loyalty, trustworthiness; the opposite of *perfidy*. Many banks or financial institutions have the word *fidelity* in their name: "I know I can count on my partner's *fidelity*." (-*ity* = noun form)

Root
fid means "trust" or "faith."

confide – to share secrets with, to have faith in: "She could *confide* anything to her mother." (*con-* = with)

confidant /kan fuh dont/ – a person in whom you can confide: "Her mother was her *confidant*." (-*ant* = person who)

confident /kan fuh dent/ – feeling certainty or confidence: "He was *confident* that he would be on time." "She was *confident* that her mother would not tell anybody." (-*ent* = inclined to)

affidavit – a sworn statement, a legal document that you swear is true and make yourself subject to the laws of perjury: "A signed traffic ticket is an *affidavit* that your name and address are true." (*af-* = to)

diffident – lacking trust in one's own powers or opinion; sometimes seen as modesty or willingness to let others lead: "He was *diffident* and let her choose the restaurant." (*dif-* = not)

Activities

In today's newspaper, are there any stories about *perfidy*?

Pronounce aloud *confidant* and *confident*.

What profession is most apt to use the term *affidavit*?

Have you noticed anybody being *diffident*?

Syllabification for correct spelling
_____
per-fi-dy

Interminable means "without ending" or "without limit": "Boring speeches that go on and on seem *interminable*." "The plains stretched on as far as the eye could see; they were *interminable*."

terminate – to end, quit, finish: "Class terminated when the bell rang."*Terminate* also means to limit space: "The lot *terminates* at the back fence."

Root
term means "limit."

exterminate – to get rid of by killing; you can *exterminate* mice, weeds, innocent people, or a whole enemy force. (*ex-* = out of)

term – a period having definite limits. A *term* is also a word or name: "What *term* do you use to describe energetic students?"

determine – to reach a decision after thinking about it: "She *determined* that she would make every effort to win." Can also mean to settle a question of controversy: "The court *determined* that he was guilty." (*de-* = from)

indeterminable – cannot be determined; there is no way of knowing: "The amount of profit the company made was *indeterminable*." (*in-* = not)

predetermined – determined beforehand: "The outcome of the election was *predetermined* when the ballot box was stuffed." (*pre-* = before)

terminology – words or terms used in a particular field: "Biology has its own *terminology*." (*-ology* = study of) (See Appendix D.)

Activities

Describe something that seemed *interminable*.

Identify some things that can *terminate*.

Name some fields of knowledge that have their own *terminology*.

Give two meanings for *term*.

Syllabification for correct spelling

in-ter-mi-na-ble

175 quadrant /kwad rant /kwod' rənt

A *quadrant* is one-fourth of a circle, an arc of 90 degrees, or a part of an area that has been divided into four parts, such as a *quadrant* of a city. A *quadrant* is also a navigation instrument that measures the angle of the sun or a star above the horizon using a quarter of a circle (0 to 90 degrees).

Root

quad means "four."

quadrangle – any four-right-angled (hence four-sided) plane figure; an area of land bounded by buildings on four sides. (-*angle* = angle)

square – a quadrangle with all four sides of equal length.

quadrennial – a period lasting four years or occurring every four years. (-*ennial* = year)

quadrillion – a very large number—a thousand followed by four sets of three zeros (1,000,000,000,000,000 or 10^{15})

quart – one fourth of a gallon; a unit of liquid measure.

quartet – a unit of four musicians; music with four parts. (-*et* = small)

quadrille – a French folk dance done with four couples.

quadruple – increase by four times as many.

quarantine – a period of isolation for persons suspected of having an infectious disease, originally lasting forty days.

quatrain – a poem with four lines, usually rhyming.

squad – the smallest army unit, originally consisting of four troops.

Activities

Draw a *quadrant*.

Draw a *quadrangle* and a *square*.

Write a *quadrillion*.

Compose an original *quatrain*.

Syllabification for correct spelling

---

quad-rant

176 radiate /ray dee ate /rā' dē āt'

Radiate means to send out light or joy: "The bride *radiated* joy and happiness as she walked down the aisle." "The electric heater in the wall *radiates* heat."

radius – a line from the center to the edge of a circle; half of the circle's diameter. The length of the circumference is the *radius* times 3.14 (pi).

radiator – something that sends out *rays* of heat, such as a wall heater in an apartment or office: "The *radiator* in a car cools the engine by *radiating* heat from the circulating fluid into the air."

Root
rad means "ray" or "spoke."

ray – beam of light or heat: "The sun's *rays* shone through the clouds." Also a *ray* is a type of flat fish.

eradiate – to send out rays; also a synonym for *radiate*.

irradiate – to illuminate; to enlighten intellectually: "Some foods are *irradiated* to keep them fresh longer." "The teacher *irradiated* wisdom." *Irradiate* can also be used as another synonym for *radiate*.

radial – arranged in a raylike pattern: "The town's main streets were *radial*; they all came together at a central point."

A similar root, *radi,* means "root" and is used in *radical* and *eradicate*.

Activities

Which three of the above words can mean about the same thing?

In a *radial* pattern of streets, how can you always get from one street to any other?

How does a car *radiator* cool the engine?

Syllabification for correct spelling

---

ra-di-ate

What can *radiate* besides heat?

177 anagram /ann uh gram /an' ə gram'

An *anagram* is a game, puzzle, or amusement in which the letters of a word are rearranged to form a new word: for example, *race* and *care*, and *rail* and *lair*. *Anagram* can also sometimes mean finding a short word within a longer word, such as *own* in *down* or *rat* in *rate*. (*ana-* = against)

It should be noted that this Greek root is the origin of the Latin root *graph*, used in many modern English words such as "telegraph"; *graph* also means "write."

Root

gram means "letter" or, more generally, something "written" or "drawn."

diagram – a sketch, plan, or graph for communicating ideas in a form beyond just words; often used in science, mathematics, and mechanics. (*dia-* = across)

epigram – a short, often witty, statement or poem, sometimes used on grave stones: "Here lies old Bill, who came here against his will." (*epi-* = upon)

grammar – the structure of a language and the rules for its correct use.

monogram – a letter or letters standing for a name and often put on paper or clothes. (*mono-* = one)

parallelogram – a geometric figure with opposite sides parallel and equal in length. (*parallel* = parallel)

program – the outline of a plan, procedure, or performance; a printed list of the acts of a play. (*pro-* = before)

gram – a unit of weight in the metric system: 1 cubic centimeter of water.

Activities

Discover some *anagrams* of your own.

Make a *diagram* of the rooms in your house.

Find or write some *epigrams*.

Draw a *parallelogram*.

Syllabification for correct spelling

an-a-gram

To *ratify* is to approve something formally, to make it legal, to confirm: "The State Department might sign a treaty, but the Senate must *ratify* it to make it an official policy of the government." "An employee might propose a deal, but the board of directors must *ratify* it if it is very large."

Root
rat means "fixed" or "determined."

ratio – the numerical relationship between two things: "The *ratio* of cats to dogs in the shelter was two to one (2:1); there were two cats for every dog."

rate – an estimate of value or quality: "How did you *rate* the performance?"; a ratio: "The tax *rate* is 8 percent of the purchase price."; to angrily scold or rebuke: "She violently *rated* against the government's policy."

ration – a fixed share: "The pirates each got a *ration* of the water." (-*ion* =noun suffix)

rational /ra' shun al/ – based on reason or common sense: "The agreement was *rational* and well thought out." (-*al* = adjective suffix)

rationale /ra shu nal'/ – the fundamental reasoning behind something: "The *rationale* for the agreement was good." (-*ale* = noun suffix)

rationalize – to explain, but often used to try to justify a questionable action: "He tried to *rationalize* why he came home late." (-*ize* = verb suffix)

Activities

How do you change *ration* from a noun into a verb?

What is the property tax *rate* in your area?

What is the *ratio* of males to females in your group or class?

What actions should parents have to *ratify*?

Syllabification for correct spelling

---

rat-i-fy

Rectitude is the quality of being straight. It can apply to a tree: "Young trees have a natural tendency toward *rectitude*; they want to grow straight up."*Rectitude* also means morally straight, honest, sticking to high standards: "Even among drug dealers there is a touch of *rectitude*, because if they lie or cheat other drug dealers, they will be shot."

> **Root**
> *rect* means "straight."

correct – without error, not wrong. (*cor-* = with)

incorrect – wrong. (*in-* = not)

direct – straight, without detour: "What is the most *direct* way to town?"; to show the way: "Can you *direct* me to city hall?"

director – a person who shows the way, such as a *play director* or a *company director;* a boss or leader. (*-or* = person who)

rector – like a director usually applied to the head person in a school, church, or religious order.

indirect – not following a straight line, roundabout.

erect – vertical in position: "The soldier stood *erect* as the officer inspected the troops."; putting up, raising: "A new building is being *erected* downtown."

rectify – to make straight: "Please *rectify* your mistakes." "The carpenter *rectified* the wall and made it straight and smooth."

Activities

Would a bank hire a person who was without *rectitude*?

Are *direct* and *indirect* antonyms (opposites)?

Is the new minister of a church likely to be called a *director* or a *rector*?

If a box is out of shape, what word would you use when speaking of making it square?

> **Syllabification for correct spelling**
> _____
> **rec-ti-tude**

Ascend means to move up, either quickly or slowly, either by stages or continuously: "The airplane *ascended* rapidly after take off." "The bright new employee with a good vocabulary is sure to *ascend* through the ranks of management." (*a-* = to)

descend – to climb or move down; the antonym of *ascend:* "You have fewer friends on the job when you are *descending* than when you are ascending." "Mountain climbers say that *descending* is more dangerous than ascending." (*de-* = down)

Root
scend means "to climb."

condescend – to be nice and polite, perhaps overly polite, to those whom you deem inferior to you: "They *condescended* to shake hands with their former enemy." (*con-* = with)

descendant – one who comes from an ancestor: "You are a *descendent* of your grandmother and of your great-grandmother." "Microbes and great teachers can have *descendants* too."

transcend – to climb over, surpass, exceed: "The runner *transcended* the pain and won the race." (*trans-* = across)

transcendental – beyond the bounds of any category or ordinary experience: "He had a *transcendental* experience watching the sunrise from the top of Mount Everest."

Activities

If you *ascend* a mountain, are you going up or down?

Would you like someone who was *condescending* to you?

Does your mother have any *descendants*? Who?

Have you had any *transcendental* experiences?

Syllabification for correct spelling
_____
as-cend

APPENDIX A

Author's Comments

This book is not remedial.

It is full-bore academic.

It is dedicated to the fact that kids are not dumb—but sometimes their curriculum is.

If the teacher doesn't learn some new words using this book, I'll be surprised. I certainly have while preparing it.

This book doesn't tell you what to do every minute or every step of the way, but it does give you a lot of vocabulary content to use as you see fit.

Each lesson can last three minutes, or much longer.

You can teach one word or the whole lesson.

You can do all the lessons or just the ones you deem suitable for your class.

Or just the ones you have time for.

You can select lessons, or parts of lessons, for small groups or even for an individual.

This book is old-fashioned. Basically, it requires a teacher to select, supplement, and add enthusiasm.

Occasionally you can just hand it to a bright, motivated student for at least a page or two.

This book might appeal to some parents for home study use, but at least your students should remember or write down some of the words to discuss or use with their parents. Let the parents know that there is something scholarly going on in school.

To know the origin and history of words is to know the history of civilization.

Learning vocabulary is a lifelong task, so start early and make it interesting and fun, because you're never done.

ESL (English as a Second Language) for Spanish-Speaking Students

Many of the words offered in this book are Latin based, and Spanish is a Latin-based language. Therefore, Spanish-speaking children will have some cultural affinity for learning these words. Many of the words also have Spanish cognates. So learning these words may improve reading, speaking, writing, and listening in both English and Spanish.

Stages in Word Learning

Learning vocabulary is incremental. Here are some of the steps:

Recognition: I think I've seen or heard this word before.

Incremental: I have a vague idea what this word means.

Denotative or dictionary meaning: I can give a fair definition and example of use of this word. Later I can give a more mature definition and example.

Polysemy: I know other (many) meanings or uses for this word.

Connotative or emotional meaning: I know some of the subtle emotional meanings.

Morphemic analysis: I know the morpheme units such as roots and prefixes.

Generalize: I know other words that use these morphemes.

Semantic networks: I know other words related in meaning to this word.

We all have four vocabularies:

1. Reading (largest)
2. Listening (next largest)
3. Speaking (smaller)
4. Writing (smallest)

Praise students often for trying out new words, even if they are not pronounced, used, or spelled exactly right.

APPENDIX B

Research

Many schools, at the urging of the federal government (National Reading Panel, 2000), want to have some research basis for the development of the curriculum materials they use. So here are the main sources used in writing this book.

Oregon Study: Frequency

Lynne Anderson-Inman and colleagues at the University of Oregon (1981) developed a list of 25,782 words that they felt should be known by a high school senior. This list was based on three classical word-frequency studies—Carroll, Davies, and Richman per website (1971); Harris and Jacobson (1972); and Thorndike and Lorge (1944)—as well as on the glossaries of 36 secondary-level textbooks.

These 25,782 words were then analyzed by morphographs (the smallest units of meaning in words; basically, roots and affixes). The words in this book include all of the roots that had 25 or more example words, and many roots that had 10 or more example words. The main or first word in each lesson was frequently one of the harder example words.

The lessons are derived from a number of other sources as well, but all of the most useful roots and their example words from the Oregon study are included in the book.

Dale and O'Rourke Study: Semantics

The Oregon Study vocabulary word list is based on word frequency counts—the counting of millions of words to determine which are the most used.

The Dale and O'Rourke study (1976) takes a different approach: that of "word meaning." Dale and O'Rourke's basic purpose was to find out what word meanings are known at each grade level. They tested thousands of words in grades 1 through 12 and classified them by their roots. They then developed three lists based on root difficulty level.

Level 1 roots: elementary, junior, and senior high school

Level 2 roots: high school and college

Level 3 roots: upper college and technical

This book includes all of Dale and O'Rourke's Level 1 and Level 2 roots with example words.

Beeler Study: Linguistics

Coming at vocabulary from yet another approach are linguistic scholars, etymologists, and classicists, such as Beeler (1988). Though short on counting and numerical tabulation, this approach is long on Latin and Greek origins of English words and on practical insights into the formation of words.

I referred to this study often, particularly for example words and meanings for roots.

Dictionaries

The main dictionary used in writing these lessons was the online *Merriam-Webster's Unabridged*. All of the main words and most of the example words were looked up for meaning. But unabridged dictionary meanings are long, sometimes going into hundreds of words in length. So I greatly shortened and simplified the definitions. Also, only main meanings, not every variation, were included.

Word pronunciation is a problem. Not everyone understands or is fluent with dictionary pronunciation systems. So I attempted to give a very informal and, I fear, somewhat inconsistent pronunciation right after each main word. For accuracy, however, I put in a formal dictionary pronunciation using the *Random House Dictionary* because it is simpler than the Merriam-Webster system and, I think, just as accurate.

I also referred often to the *Dictionary of Latin and Greek Origins* (Moore and Moore, 1997) for meaning and example words.

Book of Lists

I also frequently referred to my book *The Vocabulary Teacher's Book of Lists* (Fry, 2004), particularly for the master lists of prefixes, roots, and suffixes.

U.S. Department of Education

The U.S. Department of Education has funded a number of vocabulary studies (see http://www.ed.gov/rschstat). Both the synthesis of many studies by the National Reading Panel and the No Child Left Behind Act advocate "direct instruction of vocabulary," "specific word instruction," and "word learning strategies."

This book certainly meets U.S. and most states' standards for both direct and specific word instruction. It also teaches a major learning strategy of encouraging the students to search for meaning units (morphemes) in new words.

Prefix Spelling Variations

Prefixes are very useful meaning units (morphemes); however:

1. Sometimes one prefix can have *two different meanings:*

    in- = "not" as in *inconsistent*

    in- = "to" or "into" as in *include*

2. Sometimes one prefix can be *spelled two or more ways:*

    con- = "with" or "together" as in *concentrate*

    co- = "with" or "together" as in *cohabit*

3. Sometimes the *Prefix Double-Letter Rule* takes effect. According to this rule the first letter of the root becomes the last letter of the prefix, giving the word a double letter. For example:

    prefix *ad-*, meaning "to" or "toward," as in *admit,* becomes *ac-* in *accident* and *af-* in *affix*

Prefix *a-*

Meaning: "on," as in *afoot, ashore, aboard*

Meaning: "not," as in *apathy, apolitical, atypical*

Prefix *ad-*

Meaning: "to" or "toward"

   1st spelling: *ad-*, as in *admit, adverse*

   2nd spellings—Prefix Double-Letter Rule:

   ab-, as in *abbreviate*

ac-, as in *accident, accord*

af-, as in *affluent, affix*

ag-, as in *aggrandize, aggregate*

al-, as in *allege, alliance*

am-, as in *ammeter, ammunition*

an-, as in *annex, annual*

ap-, as in *applause, appeal*

ar-, as in *arrest, arrive*

as-, as in *asset, associate*

at-, as in *attach, attire*

3rd spelling: *ad-* becomes *ac-* before roots beginning with the /k/ sound (letters *c, k,* and *q*); for example, *accurate, acknowledge, acquaint*

Prefix *an-*

Meaning: "not," as in *anemia, anarchy, anesthetic*

Meaning: "to," as in *annex, annual, announce*

Prefix *co-*

Meaning: "with"

1st spelling: *co-*, as in *cohabit, coherence, cooperate*

2nd spellings—Prefix Double-Letter Rule:

col-, as in *collate, college, collect*

cor-, as in *correct, corrupt, correlate*

3rd spelling: *con-*, as in *conceivable, concession, concentration*

4th spelling: *com-*, as in *complain, compare, committee*

Prefix *de-*

Meaning: "down," as in *deject, denounce, degenerate*

Meaning: "away"

1st spelling: *de-*, as in *delude, defame, deduct*

2nd spelling: *di-*, as in *diversion*

Prefix *ex-*

Meaning: "out of"

1st spelling: *ex-*, as in *excess, exit, exact*

2nd spelling: *e-*, as in *eject, elude, emit*

3rd spelling—Prefix Double-Letter Rule: *ef-*, as in *efface, effluent, efficient*

Prefix *in-*

Meaning: "in" or "into"

1st spelling: *in-*, as in *inhale, incline, include*

2nd spelling: *en-*, as in *encircle, encourage, enact*

3rd spelling: *em-*, as in *embalm, embarrass, empower*

Meaning: "not"

1st spelling: *in-*, as in *inactive, inaccurate*

2nd spelling: *im-*, as in *imprison, impartial*

3rd spellings—Prefix Double-Letter Rule:

il-, as in *illegal, illegible*

im-, as in *immerse, immoral, immortal*

ir-, as in *irreligious, irrational*

Prefix *sub-*

Meaning: "under"

1st spelling: *sub-*, as in *submarine, submit, subsidize*

2nd spellings—Prefix Double-Letter Rule:

suc-, as in *success*

suf-, as in *suffer*

sug-, as in *suggest*

sup-, as in *support*

sur-, as in *surreal*

APPENDIX D

Useful Roots for Scholarly Words

Make these roots into *a person* by changing the suffix into *-ist.* For example: *anthropologist, archaeologist*

Make these roots into *a fear* by changing the suffix into *-phobia.* For example: *anthrophobia, archaephobia*

Make these roots into *a love of* by changing the suffix into *-philia.* For example: *anthrophilia, archaephilia*

-ology words (meaning science of or study of)

anthropology: humans

archaeology: ancient culture

astrology: stars (fortune-telling)

astronomy: stars (science)

audiology: hearing

bacteriology: bacteria

biology: life

biotechnology: using living organisms to make or improve things

cardiology: heart

chronology: time

cosmetology: cosmetics

criminology: crime

dermatology: skin

ecology: environment

endocrinology: glands

enterology: intestines

entomology: insects

etymology: word history, origin

gastroenterology: stomach, bowel

genealogy: ancestors, relationships

geology: earth

gerontology: aging

gynecology: women

hagiology: holy saints

hematology: blood

hydrology: water

ichythyology: fish

lexicology: words

meteorology: weather

microbiology: small life

morphology: forms of life

musicology: music

mythology: myths

neology: new words

neurology: nerves

numerology: numbers (fortune-telling)

ontology: existence

ophthalmology: eyes

ornithology: birds

otolaryngology: ear, nose, throat

otology: ears

paleontology: antiquities

petrology: rocks

pharmacology: drugs

philology: love of words

phraseology: style—of speaking and writing

psychology: mind

pterodology: ferns

radiology: radiation

seismology: quake—earthquakes

sociology: society

technology: skill—applied science

terminology: terms

thanatology: death

thaumatology: miracles

theology: God

toxicology: poisons

urology: urine (tract)

zoology: animals

REFERENCES

Anderson-Inman, L., Dixon, R., and Becker, W. *Morphographs: An Alphabetical List with Exemplars.* Technical Report 1981-1. Eugene: University of Oregon, College of Education, 1981.

Beeler, D. *Book of Roots; A Full Study of Our Families of Words.* Homewood, IL: Union Representative, 1988.

Carroll, J. B., Davies, P., and Richman, B. *American Heritage Word Frequency Book.* Boston: Houghton Mifflin, 1971.

Cunningham, A. E. "Vocabulary Growth Through Independent Reading and Reading Aloud to Children." In E. Hiebert and M. Kamil, *Teaching and Learning Vocabulary.* Mahwah, NJ: Earlbaum, 2005.

Dale, E., and O'Rourke, J. *The Living Word Vocabulary: The Words We Know.* Elgin, IL: Dome, 1976.

Fry, E. *The Vocabulary Teacher's Book of Lists.* San Francisco: Jossey-Bass, 2004.

Harris, A. J., and Jacobson, M. D. *Basic Elementary Reading Vocabularies.* New York: Macmillan, 1972.

Moore, B., and Moore, M. *Dictionary of Latin and Greek Origins: A Comprehensive Guide to the Classical Origins of English Words.* Chicago: NTC Publishing Group, 1997.

National Reading Panel. *Report of the National Reading Panel: Reports of the Subgroups.* Washington, DC: National Institute of Child Health and Human Development Clearinghouse, 2000.

Stein, J. (Ed.). *The Random House Dictionary of the English Language.* New York: Random House, 1973.

Thorndike, E. L., and Lorge, I. *The Teacher's Word Book of 30,000 Words.* New York: Teacher's College Press, Columbia University, 1944.

Webster's Third New International Dictionary, Unabridged. Springfield, MA: Merriam-Webster, 2002. Available at http://unabridged.merriam-webster.com

INDEX

(Note: Numbers in this index refer to lesson numbers. The underlined word is the key word of each lesson.)

superlative degree, 2
supernatural, 80
supersonic, 112
supervene, 44
support, 63
sur-, 103, 149
surmount, 103
surpass, 149
sus-, 101
sustain, 101
sustenance, 101
sym-, 22, 65, 77
symbol, 77
sympathy, 7, 22, 65
syn-, 7, 37, 77, 111
synchronized, 111
synonyms, 46
tacit, 46
taciturn, 46
tain, 101
taint, 101
tant, 21, 103
tantalize, 21
tantalum, 21
tantamount, 21, 103
Taoism, 28
tele-, 45, 78, 100
telephone, 100
telescope, 45
television, 78
ten, 79, 145
tenant, 145
tend, 148
tenet, 145
tent, 145
term, 174
terminate, 174
terminology, 174
terra-, 67
theocracy, 36
therm, 79
thermodynamics, 79
thermometer, 79
thermostat, 79
-thesis, 37
-tion, 80, 136
tom, 61

tomy, 61
ton, 116
tone, 116
tonic, 116
tonsillectomy, 61
tor, 115
torch, 115
tort, 115
torture, 115
torque, 115
tra-, 117
tract, 70
traction, 70
tractor, 70
trade, 1
trans-, 63, 71, 112, 117,
    138, 141, 152, 169, 180
transact, 150
transcend, 180
transcendental, 180
transfusion, 169
transistor, 138
transmissible, 152
transmit, 71
transonic, 112
transport, 63
transpose, 141
transvestite, 117
travesty, 117
trespass, 149
tri, 6, 64
triad, 6
triangle, 6
tribe, 6, 151
tribune, 151
tribut-, 128
tributary, 128
tribute, 128
trident, 6
trop, 58
-trophy, 79
troposphere, 58
turb, 13
turbid, 13
turbine, 13
turbulent, 13
typhoon, 64

-ular, 81
ultimate, 120
ultimatum, 120
ultra-, 120
ultramicro, 120
ultrasound, 120
un-, 7, 62, 108, 142
undercover, 154
undertone, 116
undisciplined, 114
undisturbed, 13
unemphatic, 7
unendurable, 108
unequivocally, 7
ungrateful, 23
uni-, 64, 68, 87, 124
unicorn, 68
uniform, 124
unincorporated, 38
unique, 68
universal, 68, 87
universe, 68
university, 68, 87
unjustified, 60
unsociable, 97
-ure, 80, 98
vac-, 1
vacation, 1
vail-, 4
valedictorian, 29
valid, 29
value, 4
vari, 118
variable, 118
variance, 118
variant, 84, 118
variegated, 118
variety, 118
vary, 118
ven, 44
ventriloquist, 170
ver, 41
verdict, 41
vers, 87, 88
versatile, 87
verse-, 68
vert, 88